FOCUS ON

STAMPS

FOCUS ON

STAMPS

MICHAEL BRIGGS

HAMLYN

ACKNOWLEDGEMENTS

Most of the photographs in this book were specially taken for the Octopus Publishing Group by David Johnson - the stamps were supplied by Stanley Gibbons Ltd or from the author's collection, unless otherwise credited below. The publishers would like to thank Tristan Brittain of Stanley Gibbons Ltd for the loan of the Irish £1 forgery on page 51; Malcolm Sprei of M&S Stamps, 77 The Strand, London for the propaganda forgery on page 50; Stanley Gibbons Ltd, 399 the Strand, London for the equipment, albums and catalogues on pages 14-21 and 24; and the following individuals and organizations for permission to reproduce the pictures in this book; Ancient Art & Architecture collection/Ronald Sheridan 54 top left. Stanley Gibbons Ltd 32 top, 33, 46 top left and right, 47 top left, right and centre, 49 centre, 50 bottom, 52 top, 53 top left, 54 right, 54-55, 56 upper and lower centre, 56 bottom, 57 top and upper centre, 59 bottom left, 62 top and bottom right, 64 top left, 65 top, 65 upper and lower centre left, French Picture Library/Barrie Smith 11 bottom centre, 12 top and bottom. Magnum/Erich Lessing 55 bottom left; Mann Hughes Gerrish Ltd/Royal Mail Stamps 68. National Postal Museum, London/Othens 49 top right, 50 upper and lower centre, 62 lower centre, 62 bottom left. Judy Todd 11 bottom left. John Walmsley 9 bottom right. ZEFA 11 top left, centre and right, 11 bottom right, 13 left and right.

Illustrators:
Peter Bull Art: maps (72-75). **David Ashby (Garden Studio):** all other diagrams and artwork.

Editor: Andrew Farrow
Series Designer: Anne Sharples
Picture Researcher: Judy Todd
Production Controller: Linda Spillane

This edition first published in 1995 by
Hamlyn Children's Books,
an imprint of Reed Children's Books,
Michelin House, 81 Fulham Road, London SW3 6RB,
and Auckland, Melbourne, Singapore and Toronto

ISBN 0 600 57369 9 (hb)
ISBN 0 600 58788 6 (pb)

A CIP catalogue record for this book is available
at the British Library.

Printed in Great Britain

CONTENTS

Stamp Collecting 8
Where to Obtain Stamps 10
Albums 14
Equipment 16
Care of Stamps 20
Displaying Stamps 22
Catalogues 24
Types of Stamp 28
Valuable Stamps 32
Unusual Stamps 34
Collecting By Country 36
Collecting By Theme 40
Variations on a Theme 44
How Stamps are Made 46
Forgeries and Fakes 50
Mistakes 52
Early Postal Systems 54
Airmail 56
Unusual Postal Services 58
First Day Covers 60
Postmarks 62
Overprints 64
Cinderellas 66
Stamp Clubs 68
Foreign Alphabets 70
Stamp Maps 72
Index 76

STAMP COLLECTING

Stamp collecting is one of the most popular hobbies in the world. Nobody knows for sure how many collectors there are. A British Royal Mail survey suggests that some 4 million people in Britain (of a population of about 55 million) collect stamps in some way - many of them, perhaps, just buying the new issues that appeal to them.

THE FIRST OF MANY

The first adhesive postage stamp was issued by Britain in 1840 as a convenient way of showing that postage had been paid by the sender of a letter. This was part of a wider reform of the government-run postal system - letters were now charged by weight rather than by the distance they travelled - that led to a cheaper and more efficient service.

STAMPS AROUND THE WORLD

The idea of the postage stamp soon found favour in other countries, too. It was not long before people began to collect these tiny, usually exotic, pieces of paper from distant parts of the world. By the 1860s, famous names such as Stanley Gibbons in England, John Scott in the USA and Theodore Champion in France began to trade in stamps and to produce the first albums and catalogues. Stamp collecting caught the imagination of young and old, and the ordinary and the famous: President Roosevelt of the USA and King George V of Britain were keen collectors.

Today, collectors have a huge choice, because many hundreds of stamps are issued each year by almost every country in the world. These give a fascinating insight into many cultures, depicting landscapes and buildings, sport, wildlife, transport, art, scientific achievement and many other things - in fact, there are few subjects that have not appeared on stamps. All of this is captured on tiny pieces of paper, many of which are works of art in themselves.

Stamp dealer Theodore Champion and stamp production are shown on these two stamps (left).

STUDYING STAMPS

It is not until you begin to study stamps closely, to ask why and how they were produced, that you can call yourself a philatelist. A philatelist is someone who studies stamps, rather than just collects them. (The word philately, meaning stamp collecting, is derived from the Greek word *ateles*, meaning 'tax-free'.) You can study the stamps of a single country, discovering why they were issued and how they were printed, or, perhaps, delve into its postal history. Whatever you start to collect, you will soon discover why stamps have such worldwide appeal.

A Swedish stamp booklet (top) shows some of the many ways of transporting mail. The booklet from the USA (above) promotes a stamp exhibition - an ideal place to buy, see and learn about stamps.

Postal history (above) and stamp collecting (above right) are popular subjects for stamps.

STAMP COLLECTING

You can devote as little or as much time to stamp-collecting as you wish. Of course, enthusiastic younger stamp collectors won't be able to collect some of the more expensive or rare stamps, but this won't reduce their enjoyment of the hobby. As with any activity, there is no substitute for help and guidance from experienced collectors - hopefully, this book will point you in the right direction. And it is also worth joining a local stamp club, because most experienced philatelists will be only too pleased to aid the young collector with advice and assistance.

Many collectors like to buy stamps by post, because it gives them more time, at home, to decide what they want for their collection. Never be hasty when looking at stamps. Sometimes you will find interesting postmarks or stamped messages on the envelopes.

WHERE TO OBTAIN STAMPS

You may start to collect stamps when someone gives you a packet of stamps or a starter pack as a present. Perhaps you are attracted by colourful stamps on letters sent by friends from overseas. However you begin, you will want to buy stamps, to start or add to your collection, to fill gaps in a set or to start a new country. There are many ways of doing this.

STAMP PACKETS

Packets of stamps are widely available. They range in content from just a few stamps from a single country or subject to packets containing many hundreds of stamps from around the world. They are ideal for starting a collection - whether a general one, a single country or on a theme or subject - because you can obtain a large number of stamps, usually all different, quite cheaply.

KILOWARE

Kiloware, which is a quantity of stamps cut from their envelopes and sold by weight, is another way to begin a collection. Usually sold unsorted, there is always the chance of finding some scarcer stamps, though there will be many of the more common sort, as well as damaged and heavily postmarked copies. You will need to sort them out carefully and prepare them by floating off the backing paper (see page 20) before they can be mounted in your album. Kiloware is also likely to contain many duplicate stamps: these can be swapped with your stamp-collecting friends - yet another way of obtaining stamps.

Stamp packets (above) and kiloware (below) are easy ways of building up a stamp collection.

STAMP DEALERS

If you are lucky enough to have a stamp shop near where you live, you can quite easily go there and look at the dealer's stock. You will be able to obtain advice there as well. Stamp fairs are held in many places, either on a regular basis or perhaps as a special event organized by the local stamp club. You will find at least half a dozen stamp dealers, offering a wide choice of material, at these fairs.

Many stamp dealers sell by post: a glance through one of the monthly stamp magazines available at your newsagent or local library will reveal dealers offering everything from cheap packets and sets to scarce, and expensive, single stamps.

Stamps sent to you 'on approval' are another way of buying by post. Just select and pay for those you have decided to buy and return those you don't want.

LOOKING AT POSTAL HISTORY

Postal history is the study of all aspects of a postal system and its development. It forms an important background to stamp-collecting and has many fascinating sidelines. For example, postboxes - the first roadside postbox for the collection of letters was introduced in Paris in 1653 - can be found in many different styles. There is even a club for those who are interested in them. Some unusual boxes from around the world are shown below.

A box from Budapest, Hungary.

This ornate box is from Germany.

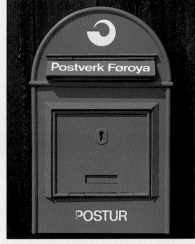

A wall box from the Faroe Islands.

A modern French box with two slots for local and longer-distance letters.

An Indian pillar box.

This two-slot box is from Hong Kong.

POST OFFICES

One important source of stamps if you collect those of your own country is your local post office. Many larger post offices have a special section devoted to the needs of collectors, though you will, of course, only be able to buy new and recent issues there. Most overseas post offices, too, provide a postal service for collectors, enabling them to receive new items as they are issued. Write to the Philatelic Bureau of your home postal authority for details of its services, sending a self-addressed envelope for the reply.

STAMP CLUBS

All keen stamp collectors should belong to a stamp club. Another chapter in this book (page 68) will tell you something about the different types of club and the advantages of membership. A major advantage, of course, is the opportunity to exchange stamps with fellow members. Many clubs run an 'exchange packet' through which members can sell their stamps. The packet is passed from one person to the next, by hand or post. It also gives those unable to attend meetings regularly a chance to buy and sell stamps.

Stamp vending machines (right) often provide stamps that you cannot buy at the post office counter. This machine from the USA (right) has a wide choice of stamps.The Danish machine (far right) is sited next to a post box; it sells stamp booklets.

COLLECTOR'S HINT
Don't forget to take your tweezers when you go to a dealer. A pocket stockbook in which to keep your purchases, and a magnifying glass, will be useful, too.

You can buy stamps at post offices (above). Many have special sections for collectors. Street markets, too, are a source of stamps; some, like this French one (right), are devoted just to collectors' needs.

EXHIBITIONS

Stamp exhibitions provide an excellent opportunity to buy stamps from a wide range of dealers gathered together under one roof. Small exhibitions are held throughout the country, and they are advertised in stamp magazines and locally. Larger, national, shows are held, too. For example, 'Stampex' is held twice a year in London (spring and autumn), and there are usually a hundred or more dealers there.

On an even larger scale are the 'Internationals'. Collectors from all over the world display their stamps, and many overseas postal administrations and stamp dealers attend, too. Britain holds an international exhibition every 10 years. The last was in 1990 and celebrated the 150th anniversary of the Penny Black.

AUCTIONS

One other method of obtaining stamps should be mentioned: the stamp auction. Auctions range from those containing cheaper sets and single stamps, to sales of a valuable specialized collection. All auctions have a catalogue describing the lots (items) on offer and giving an idea of how much money they are expected to fetch. They also provide details of how to bid. Collectors do not have to attend an auction in person, because bids can be placed by post. Most auctions are for experienced collectors only.

BUYING STAMPS

Keep an up-to-date list of the items you want for your collection. Without one, it is very easy to buy a stamp that you own already.

Examine stamps and envelopes carefully before you buy them. Check for small tears, missing perforations, staining and other damage.

Don't forget to look at the back of stamps, especially if buying unmounted ones. Faults often show up better from the back of a stamp than from the front.

ALBUMS

It is not until your stamps are sorted and arranged in some sort of order that they become a proper stamp collection. The easiest way of doing this is to keep them in a stamp album.

PRINTED ALBUMS

The simplest type of album contains pages with printed headings for each country. Some have their pages bound like a book; others have loose leaves, allowing you to add pages as your collection grows.

Sooner or later, if you collect stamps from the whole world, you will decide to concentrate your collection on the stamps of just one country or area. If you are a one-country collector, you can choose to use one of the many printed albums available. These have a printed space for each stamp issued. All that needs to be done is to mount the stamp in the correct place. However, you will probably find that there are some spaces you will never fill.

BLANK ALBUMS

For most serious collectors, the blank loose-leaf album is the best choice. This contains pages printed with a feint grid to help in the arrangement of your stamps. There are many different types and sizes available: the larger ones are better for displaying blocks and longer sets of stamps.

Albums with blank pages enable you to arrange your collection just as you want it. You don't have to follow any particular arrangement, and it means you can include whatever write-up you wish. A blank album is almost essential for a person who collects themes rather than countries.

Leaves should be chosen with care. A shiny, soft paper is likely to tear when a stamp is removed from it, so a smooth, hard surface is better. Some leaves have a transparent paper leaf attached over them. This helps to protect stamps from damage.

OTHER ALBUMS

Special albums are made to hold first day covers, postcards and stamp booklets. These have leaves of transparent plastic pockets into which the item is slipped for protection. Stockbook-type albums contain pages with transparent strips attached to them. The stamps are placed behind the strips and there is no need to use a stamp hinge or protective mount. Pages with different numbers and sizes of strip are available, allowing different-sized items to be held safely. A small stockbook is handy for holding your duplicate stamps or for stamps waiting to be mounted in your album.

Blank loose-leaf albums (above and left) allow you to mount stamps as you wish, and to include notes and other items in your collection. Printed albums (below left) are better for beginners or for straight-forward collections.

COLLECTOR'S HINT
Never put too many pages in an album, especially a springback type, because the binding mechanism could be weakened. Always store your albums upright, not on their sides.

TYPES OF ALBUM

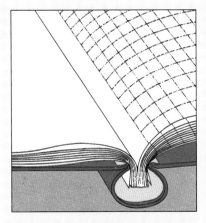

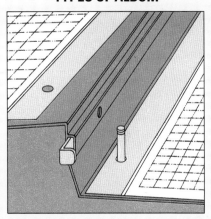

The traditional album binder is the springback. A concealed spring in the spine holds the leaves in place. One disadvantage is that the leaves do not lie flat when the album is open: they need to be removed when you are working on the collection. The leaves are removed by folding back the cover against the spring.

The pegfitting album holds punched leaves on two pegs. It has a locking mechanism which secures the binder cover to the pegs. Like the springback album, the leaves do not always lay completely flat when the album is open. Leaves hinged with a linen cloth are sometimes used to make the pages lay flatter.

Perhaps the album most popular with collectors is the ringfitting type. The number of rings varies from two to 22. The ones with lots of rings are best as the pages are less likely to tear away from the binding rings. The pages will lie flat wherever the album is opened, and they can be removed very easily.

EQUIPMENT

Stamp collecting requires very little equipment. However, as well as albums and catalogues (see page 24), a few items *are* essential. These basic items are readily available from shops or by mail order from magazines, and they need not be expensive. You are not a proper collector without them.

TWEEZERS

Stamps are fragile things and can easily be damaged if you pick them up with your fingers. Tweezers, the stamp collector's most important tool, will enable you to handle your stamps without fear of damage. Many types of tweezer are available, from fine rounded points to broad 'spade' ends. Choose the type that suits you best; make sure, however, to buy a pair intended for use with stamps. Using tweezers will probably seem strange at first, but after a little while you will handle them with ease.

MAGNIFYING GLASS

A magnifying glass will enable you to examine the fine detail of a stamp's design, detecting errors and varieties and helping to identify methods of printing. A wide range of magnifying glasses is available, from large hand-held types to small folding versions that will fit easily into your pocket. Their magnification varies, too, so try out a few different glasses to see which will be best for your needs - a fairly low-powered glass will be suitable for most work. Choose one that gives a clear, undistorted field of view.

PERFORATION GAUGE

A stamp's value may be increased if its perforation - the tiny holes around its edge used as a means of separating one stamp from another – is different from normal. A perforation gauge will help you to measure these differences. The perforation number is found by counting the number of holes in a length of 2 cm. By matching the perforations on the stamp with the dots on the card or plastic gauge, you can discover the correct perforation measurement. These gauges usually give measurements in half steps. A more complex gauge is printed with fine lines instead of dots and allows a more precise measurement.

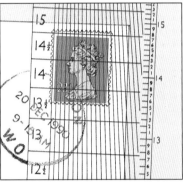

USING A PERFORATION GAUGE

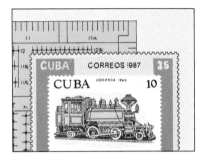

Align the perforation holes on the stamp with the dots on the gauge: when they match, you have the correct measurement. Most gauges show measurements as small as half a perforation. You should round up other fractions: for example, a measurement of between 13 and 13½ is rounded up to 13½.

This gauge enables you to obtain a more precise measurement. The stamp is moved down the gauge until the lines cut through the centres of the perforation holes; the figures on the right then give the stamp's perforation. A transparent gauge lets you measure stamps that are still on an envelope or mounted in your stamp album.

A stamp with the same measurements on all four sides (say 13) is said to be perf 13. Often the top and bottom measurements are different to those at the sides, in which case the top measurement is given first. Perf 14 x 15, for example, indicates a measurement of 14 at the top and bottom and 15 at the sides.

COLLECTOR'S HINT
When measuring the perforations of a lot of stamps, it is easier and quicker to compare them with a stamp that has already been measured. Use the perforation gauge to measure any that do not match.

OTHER EQUIPMENT

In shops and magazines you will see some other equipment for sale. None of the items shown here are particularly expensive, but only experienced collectors really need to buy them.

WATERMARK DETECTORS

Just as a difference in perforation can change the value of a stamp, so can a difference of watermark. A watermark is a deliberate thinning of the paper during its manufacture to form a design or pattern. This acts as a security device, which makes stamps more difficult to forge.

Watermarks can often be seen by holding the stamp to the light or by placing it face down on a dark surface. However, many modern stamps are printed on thick, coated paper that makes the watermark difficult to see. Therefore, various watermark detectors are available to help solve this problem. Some of them even make it possible to find a watermark on a stamp still stuck to its envelope.

PEN AND STENCIL

Although not essential items in the stamp collector's kit, a lettering stencil and pen can be useful for adding neat notes to your collection.

COLOUR GUIDES

Variations in the colour of a stamp can also make a difference to its value. Trying to judge between different shades without help can be very difficult; a colour guide is often useful.

Some guides are rather like a paint chart, although a better type has the colours printed on narrow strips of card, rather like a fan. A hole punched through each colour means the fan can be placed over the stamp for easy matching. Working in good daylight from a north-facing window is best for accurate colour matching.

ULTRAVIOLET LAMPS

An ultraviolet (UV) lamp can be useful in detecting the phosphorescent inks and papers used on many stamps. Bands of almost invisible phosphor ink aid the sorting of mail by machine, because the machines are set up to detect the position of the phosphorescence. These bands can often be seen by holding the stamp at a slight angle against a light source, but a UV lamp makes their detection much easier. You will need to be an experienced philatelist before you require a UV lamp. Skill is needed in knowing what to look for, and great care must be taken in using a lamp - looking directly at UV light can damage your eyes very seriously.

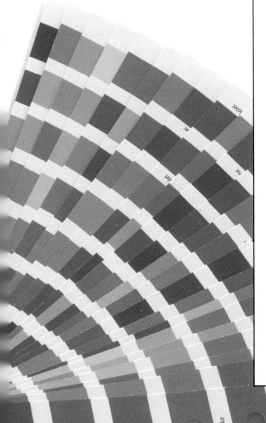

WATERMARKS AND BANDS

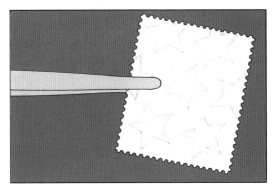

Some watermarks show up well on a dark surface or when the stamp is held up to the light. Before you try detecting watermarks, use a stamp catalogue to give an idea of the patterns you are looking for.

Holding a stamp at a slight angle to a light source can reveal phosphor bands. They show up as a dull strip on the stamp's surface.

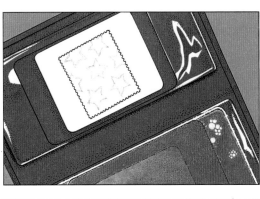

If simple methods fail to reveal the expected watermark, try using a watermark detector. First, the stamp is placed on the detector's glass block, and a sachet containing a special 'ink' is placed over it.

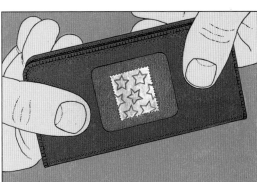

Applying pressure to the sachet reveals the watermark as a pattern in the 'ink'. It will probably take a little practice before you get used to using a detector like this.

CARE OF STAMPS

Stamps are easily damaged and should be treated with care. Always use stamp tweezers when handling them. Unless they are very rare and unusual, stamps that have been torn, creased or stained, and those that are heavily postmarked, should be thrown away - they have no value and will spoil the appearance of your collection.

PREPARING STAMPS

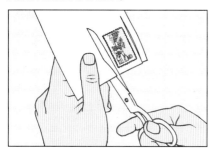

Unless you wish to keep the postmark intact, stamps cut from envelopes should be removed from the paper before being mounted in your album. First, cut the paper close to the stamps.

Next, put some warm water in a bowl and then float the cut stamps on the surface of the water *stamp side up* until the backing separates from the stamps. Remember, wet stamps are very fragile.

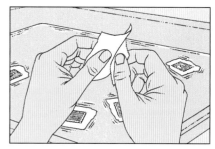

It may take some time for a stamp's gum to become wet enough for it to separate from the paper. Do *not* be tempted to give a helping hand by pulling the paper from the stamp.

A stamp may still have some of its original gum on the back. To remove it, gently wash it off with a clean paint brush dipped in clean, warm water. Stamps should be placed on clean white blotting paper or kitchen towel to dry.

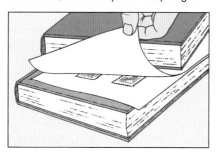

Let the stamps dry naturally, away from strong heat. They might curl slightly while drying. It is best to press them carefully between two sheets of blotting paper placed between a couple of heavy books, *after* they have dried.

COLLECTOR'S HINT
When floating stamps, put those on coloured envelopes to one side. These should be treated separately in case the colour runs when the piece is immersed in the water.

Stockbooks are useful for storing stamps. Keep your stockbook and albums in a clean, dry place.

MOUNTING STAMPS

When prepared, your stamps can be mounted on your album pages with stamp hinges. These are small, gummed pieces of transparent paper made for just this purpose. When dry, they can be peeled off the page and stamp without damaging them. Never be tempted to use other forms of adhesive paper, because you will damage your stamps. An alternative method, ideal if you do not wish to disturb the gum on the back of a stamp, is to use a protective mount. The stamp is slipped between two pieces of plastic which have been welded together on one or two sides. When the mount is stuck to the album page, the stamp remains fully protected. Protective mounts come either in strips to cut to the size you require or already cut to fit some standard stamp sizes.

If you are not ready to mount your stamps, store them in a stockbook. These come in many sizes and have strips on each page. The stamps are held safely behind the strips until they are needed.

USING PROTECTIVE MOUNTS

Protective mounts are useful for displaying mint stamps, whose value might be reduced by hinging them. They are available in black and clear forms.

Using a protective mount. It is stuck in the album by moistening its gummed back. A small guillotine makes cutting strips quick and accurate.

Inserting a mint stamp into a double-sealed mount. Although they are more expensive than hinges, you can use protective mounts to display all of your mint stamps.

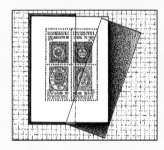

Two strips can be overlapped to mount large items, and hold them securely. Photograph corners can be used to hold first day covers.

USING A STAMP HINGE

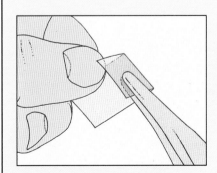

Fold over a third of the hinge, gummed side out. Some hinges are sold ready-folded.

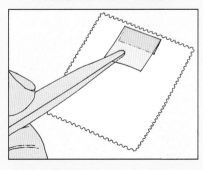

Lightly moisten the smaller portion of the hinge and place it at the top of the stamp.

Moisten the lower part of the free end of the hinge and place the stamp in position on the album page.

DISPLAYING STAMPS

How you arrange your stamps, and what additional information is included on the page, will depend very much on the kind of collection you are forming. Whether your collection is a simple 'one of everything' type, highly specialized or thematic, it should be neat and tidy.

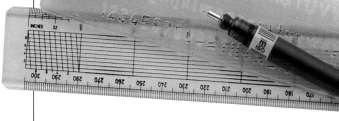

Focus On Stamps

FOCUS ON STAMPS

FOCUS ON STAMPS

Focus On Stamps

Focus On Stamps

Chagall : The Married Couple of the Eiffel Tower   Seurat : The Circus   Toulouse-La du 'Sta

Braque : The Messenger   Cezanne : The Card Playe

De La Fresnaye : 14th July   Dufy : The Red Violin

Rousseau : Old Juniet's Trap

WRITING

Most blank album pages are printed with a feint grid to aid the arrangement of your stamps. The grid will also help keep any writing straight and neat. Writing should be kept to a minimum: the stamps must be the most important items on the page. Keep any writing small, and make sure it is easily read.

Writing is best done with a fine-nibbed pen. Use black ink, because this always looks best. Do not use ball-points, because the ink forms blobs that will smudge across your stamps. Stencils or a typewriter are other methods you might prefer to use. Why not have a few practice runs to see which you find best?

DESIGNING THE PAGE

Before mounting your stamps or beginning to write anything, arrange the stamps loosely on the page. Move them about until you get a pleasing display, remembering to leave space for any writing. The positions of the stamps can then be marked lightly with a pencil, written information added, and the stamps mounted in their marked positions.

Most collectors keep to a symmetrical arrangement of their stamps: the left side of the page matches the right side. Nevertheless, thematic displays, which often contain stamps of different shapes and sizes as well as covers, postmarks and other items, often look better without such a formal style. In country collections, sets of stamps are usually arranged in value order, though it is sometimes necessary to break this order to obtain a balanced page, especially if they contain different shapes and sizes. Arranging your stamps on an album page can be a very rewarding task. A neat and tidy collection, logically arranged, will give great pleasure to you and others who see it.

These French Art stamps have a symmetrical arrangement. They are mounted neatly on the page with enough space for a brief caption beneath each stamp. The other page is not so neat - the stamps are not straight.

COLLECTOR'S HINT
A simple 'ruler' can be made from a strip of card to help you locate a page's centre or other points easily and quickly. This is a great help in positioning stamps.

PLANNING THE PAGE

Before you mount your stamps, arrange them loosely on the page, leaving space for any writing.

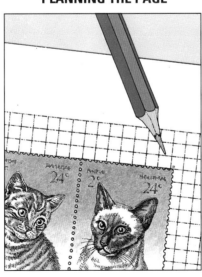

When you like the arrangement, mark the positions of the stamps with a light pencil dot by their corners.

After writing any notes on the page, the stamps can be mounted in their correct places.

CATALOGUES

A stamp catalogue is an essential item in the stamp collector's 'tool kit', because it gives details of why and when stamps were issued. It will show you what other stamps you need for your collection and give an indication of what they will cost.

TYPES OF CATALOGUE

There are many types of catalogue available. They may, like Stanley Gibbons' *Stamps of the World*, provide a listing of stamps that differ only in appearance, ignoring things such as watermarks and any differences in perforations. Others provide more details, listing all possible stamp variations as well as providing other useful information such as a stamp's designer and printer.

Catalogues may cover a group of related countries, such as the Central American nations, or a single country. Thematic subjects such as birds, railways and ships also have their own catalogues. Most major stamp catalogues are published at regular intervals, and some have supplements to keep the listings up to date. Information about new issues of stamps can be found in stamp magazines.

COLLECTOR'S HINT
Dates are often included in stamp designs. These can be a great help in finding stamps in the catalogue, especially if the country has issued many stamps.

USING A CATALOGUE

Always read the introduction to a stamp catalogue. This will tell you what sort of stamps are included. Most catalogues, for example, only list stamps issued by government postal administrations; privately-produced stamps are not included. Sometimes stamps which have been issued just for collectors and which serve no real postal need are listed in a special section. The introduction is also likely to explain about perforations, papers, watermarks and other items of a technical nature.

All catalogues are well-illustrated. Some just show one stamp in a set, others show all the stamps with different designs. The illustrations, together with brief descriptions of the stamps' designs, enable you to find the stamp you are looking for. The number beside each listed stamp is the catalogue number. This number is a convenient way of referring to a stamp without having to describe it in full.

Every collector needs a stamp catalogue. There are many types available. Shown here are catalogues from Britain (Stanley Gibbons), the USA (Scott), Germany (Michel) and France (Yvert et Tellier).

USING A CATALOGUE

Catalogues have illustrations and descriptions to help you find the stamp you are looking for. The stamps are usually listed in order of their date of issue, although each catalogue will have its own numbering system.

The number on the left is the 'catalogue number'. This is a simple way of describing a stamp. The stamps in this page are France 526 to 533.

The face value of the stamp.

Footnotes guide you to stamps in the same series.

Catalogue illustrations are often in black and white. The stamp's main colours are described.

The figures at the right show the catalogue prices for mint (unused) and used stamps respectively.

The design type number can be useful for finding an illustration of a stamp.

The perforation of the stamp.

The date of issue of the stamp.

1970-72. Various issues with phosphor bands on stamps' face.
Perf 14 x 13½ (10c), 14 x 13 (30c) or 13 (others).

526	10c. Yellow, brilliant blue and brown-red (three bands)	12	12
527	20c. Multicoloured (three bands)	12	12
528	30c. Emerald (one band)	15	5
529	40c. Cherry (two bands)	3.50	1.50

Starting in March 1970, Nos 526-29 were issued for use with automatic sorting machines which could separate the items of fast and slow mail. The phosphor bands react to long-wave ultraviolet light with a yellow or orange glow. *See also Nos 556 and 568.*

1970, 21 March. *412.* **150th anniversary of the discovery of Quinine.**
Designed and engraved by C. Haley. Recess. Perf 13.

530	50c. Deep green, light blue-green and magenta	25	15

1970, 21 March. *413.* **European Nature Conservation Year.**
Designed and engraved by Cami. Recess. Perf 13.

531	45c. Grey, pink and olive-green	40	15

412. Pierre-Joseph Pelletier and Joseph Bienaime Caventou with Quinine Formula

413. Flamingo

1970, 28 March. **Launch of the rocket *Diamant B* from Guyana.**
Designed and engraved by Combet. Recess. Perf 13

532	45c Blue-green	20	15

1970, 4 April. **World Health Organization 'Fight Cancer' day.**
Designed and engraved by Decaris. Recess. Perf 13.

533	40c plus 10c. Olive-brown, pink and blue	20	20

STAMP TERMS

You will come across many unfamiliar terms in stamp books, magazines and catalogues. Most of the ones that are commonly used by stamp collectors are explained elsewhere in this book: for example, the printing term 'intaglio' is explained on page 48, under 'How stamps are made'. If you need to know what a word or phrase means, you can use the index on page 76 to help you find a description of it.

On these two pages you will find some more explanations of the specialist terms that are used to describe stamps and other philatelic items, and a diagram showing what the parts of a stamp are called.

Adhesive Postage Stamp. Stamp affixed by gum, as opposed to handstamped, embossed or printed on to a postal item.

Aerogramme. Stamped postal stationery item of lightweight paper for carriage by air.

Aniline. A fugitive ink, ie one which runs when immersed in water.

Backstamp. Postmark applied to a postal item's back.

Bisect. Stamp cut in half and used at half of its original value.

Block. Four or more stamps joined together.

Bogus Stamp. One issued for a ficticious place or postal service or for political propaganda purposes.

Booklet. Small panes of stamps bound together between covers. Modern panes usually have a single pane stuck to a folded card cover.

Cachet. An inscription on a card or cover marking a special event, usually applied by handstamp.

CDS. Abbreviation for 'circular datestamp'.

Cliché. Individual 'stamp' (or other) part of a printing plate. Usually refers to stamps printed by letterpress.

Cover. An envelope or wrapper used in the post.

CTO. Abbreviation for 'cancelled to order'. These are stamps which, though cancelled, have not performed a postal service.

Die. An original engraved plate used to prepare a printing plate.

Duplex Cancellation. Postmark in which the datestamp and cancelling device form one piece.

Embossing. Method of printing where the paper is given a raised effect.

Entire. A complete envelope or other postal item.

Essay. A stamp design which has not been used, or has been used with alterations.

Facsimile. A reproduction of a genuine stamp. A facsimile is usually marked in some way and is not intended to defraud.

FDC. Abbreviation for first day cover.

Field Post Office. Post office used by troops on manoeuvres or active service.

Frank. Stamp or other mark used to show that mail should be carried without charge.

Gutter. Blank space between panes of a sheet of stamps.

Imprint. Inscription (usually the printer's name) found in the margin of a sheet of stamps or on the stamps themselves.

Jubilee Line. Coloured line found in the margins of a sheet of British stamps.

Key Plate. Plate that prints a common design for several countries. The value and name is added by the duty plate.

Key Type. Stamp printed in a common design for several countries.

Killer. Cancellation that heavily obliterates a stamp to prevent its reuse.

Miniature Sheet. A small sheet containing one or more stamps, usually with decorative margins.

Mint. Unused stamp as issued.

Mixed Franking. Cover or card with the stamps of two or more countries.

Mounted Mint. Unused stamp (mint) with hinge marks on the back.

Obsolete. Stamp no longer valid for postage.

Original Gum. Stamp possessing some of the gum present at the time of issue. Abbreviated to o.g.

Pane. Section of a sheet of stamps which is separated by margins. Also a leaf of stamps from a stamp booklet.

Paquebot. French term for Packet Boat. Describes mail posted onboard ship and later taken ashore for onward posting. Such mail often has a special cancellation.

Perfin. Stamp perforated with initials or other design, usually by a company, to prevent theft.

PHQ Card. A postcard produced by the British Post Office when new stamps are issued, reproducing the stamp designs.

Postal Fiscal. Fiscal stamp used for postage.

Pre-cancel. Stamp bearing a printed cancellation for use on bulk postings.

Prestige Booklet. Stamp booklet containing stamps and descriptions on a special subject. Often sponsored by organizations to mark an anniversary or other event.

PARTS OF A STAMP

This pair of Maltese 4c and 25c commemorative stamps shows many features commonly found on postage stamps. These two, which have different designs and values, are described as a 'se tenant' pair when joined together in this way. When 'se tenant' stamps form a complete picture it is called a 'composite design'.

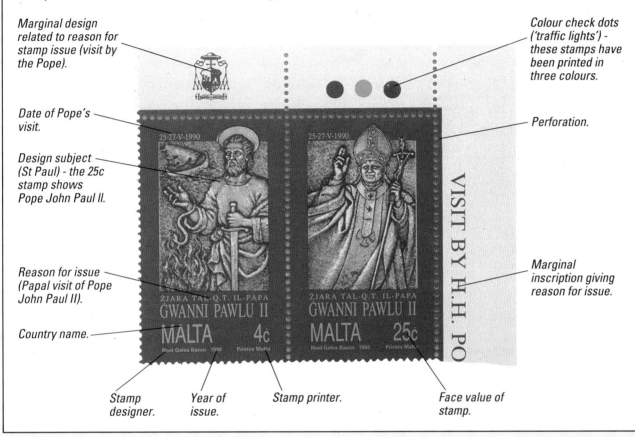

Marginal design related to reason for stamp issue (visit by the Pope).

Colour check dots ('traffic lights') - these stamps have been printed in three colours.

Date of Pope's visit.

Design subject (St Paul) - the 25c stamp shows Pope John Paul II.

Perforation.

Reason for issue (Papal visit of Pope John Paul II).

Marginal inscription giving reason for issue.

Country name.

Stamp designer.

Year of issue.

Stamp printer.

Face value of stamp.

Provisional. Stamp overprinted or surcharged for use during a temporary shortage or other emergency.

Re-entry. A doubling of the design of a line-engraved stamp (see page 48). It is caused by a new impression of the design being placed over a partly erased one.

Selvedge. The marginal paper of a sheet of stamps.

Space filler. Substandard stamp used in a collection until a better one is found.

Strip. Three or more stamps joined together in a row.

Tab. Pictorial or inscribed label attached to a stamp, particularly those of Israel.

Traffic Lights. Coloured dots found in the sheet margins of multicoloured printed stamps, one dot for each colour. They are used to check that all the colours have been printed.

Transit Mark. Postmark applied during an item's journey between point of posting and point of arrival.

Travelling Post Office. A special railway train on which mail is sorted. Mail which is posted in 'late fee' boxes on or near the train is cancelled on board with a special TPO postmark.

Universal Postal Union. A body which organizes postal co-operation between different countries. Founded in 1874, it is based in Berne, Switzerland.

Unmounted Mint. A stamp as issued which has never been hinged.

Unused. Stamp which has not passed through the post.

Used. A stamp that has been cancelled.

Vignette. The central portion of a stamp, strictly one that shades at the edges.

Wing Margin. A wide margin on some early letterpress-printed British stamps, where a gutter between stamp panes was perforated through the centre instead of near the stamp design.

TYPES OF STAMP

The first postage stamps were issued as a handy method of paying in advance - pre-paying - for the delivery of mail. Printed in sheets, in a convenient small size, most of them pictured the monarch, president or emblem of the issuing country. Their basic arrangement, or format, is still kept by many countries today, although you will also find some which are larger and with pictorial designs. These common, everyday stamps are known to collectors as definitive, permanent or regular issues.

Definitive stamps are often overlooked by many collectors, particularly when new values, watermarks, perforations or other variations appear. Once issues of such stamps are no longer available from post offices, they can be difficult to find.

CHARITY STAMPS

Charity stamps are issued by many countries. In addition to the normal postage, they carry a small extra charge (usually shown separately on the stamp) which is given to charity. Annual charity stamps have been issued by France, Germany, Switzerland, New Zealand and the Netherlands for many years.

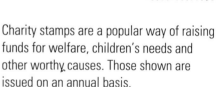

Charity stamps are a popular way of raising funds for welfare, children's needs and other worthy causes. Those shown are issued on an annual basis.

Early definitives often pictured a country's coat of arms, monarch, or president. Modern issues (left) feature a wide variety of subjects.

British regional or 'country' stamps (above) are issued for Northern Ireland, Scotland and Wales.

DEFINITIVE DESIGNS

Many countries have issued definitives in the same design for many years. Norway's Posthorn design first appeared in 1871, and variations of it were still appearing over 100 years later. Britain's 'Machin' definitives (named after the sculptor Arnold Machin whose plaster cast of the Queen's head is used as their design) were first issued in 1967. The decimal currency version of it began in 1971, and well over 150 basic variations are now listed in stamp catalogues.

BOOKLETS AND COILS

Stamp booklets and coil stamps (ones printed in long strips) are issued by many countries as a convenient way of buying stamps. Sweden's stamps are sold only in these forms.

Booklet and coil stamps often provide variations to similar stamps issued in sheets. For example, the stamps may have one or more edges that are without perforations, as with the USA example illustrated here. Also shown are South African and Swedish stamps.

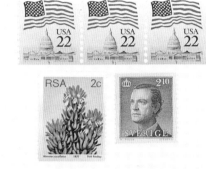

Some postage stamps are sold only in booklet form. These booklets can make a fascinating study in their own right, and many have attractive pictorial covers which can add interest to a thematic collection.

COMMEMORATIVE STAMPS

Stamps issued for special occasions probably form the largest group of stamps. Most are larger than definitives and they depict just about every subject you can think of. The first commemorative stamps issued by a government authority were those of New South Wales (Australia) in 1888 for the centenary of British settlement. Commemoratives issued by a number of countries at the same time to mark the same event are known as 'omnibus issues'. The first was issued by Portugal and its colonies in 1898. British colonies have made many such issues, the first in 1935 for King George V's Silver Jubilee. The early omnibus issues shared the same design; later ones show much more variety.

The world's first commemorative (above left) and a black-bordered 'mourning' stamp (above).

MOUNTING BOOKLETS

Some stamp booklets are quite thick and this makes them difficult to mount with photo corners. Instead, cut two vertical slits, to the height of the booklet and about 35mm apart, in the album page. Then slide the booklet's back cover between them.

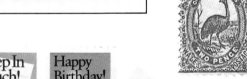

'Greetings' stamps (above) have been issued by many countries for use on personal mail.

Commemorative stamps (right) cover almost every subject you can think of - how many of these can you recognize?

AIRMAIL STAMPS

Definitives and commemoratives are not the only sorts of stamp you will come across. Stamps have been issued for many special purposes. Perhaps the most common type is the airmail stamp. Airmail stamps were particularly popular during the pioneer years of flight, when airmail routes were being developed; they often commemorated special flights. Today, when airmail is not unusual, few countries issue them. Instead, special airmail stickers and envelopes indicate that an item is to travel by air.

Airmail stamps (above) were very popular in the early years of route development. Many of them are now scarce.

Special Delivery, Parcel Post and Express stamps (above and right).

POST OFFICE SERVICES

Stamps have been issued for several other special services provided by postal authorities. Express delivery, registered mail, and delivery of newspapers, printed papers and parcels, have all been catered for. In 1913 Italy issued stamps for mail carried by a pneumatic tube system operated in several cities. Special stamps for use by government departments and by soldiers on active military service have also appeared.

'Postage due' stamps are another type of stamp you may find. They are used for collecting money from the addressee on unpaid or underpaid mail. They are also used to collect customs duties on mail sent from abroad. If you find one of these stamps on an envelope do not remove it. Left on the envelope, it will show that it has performed the service for which it was issued, and will be an interesting addition to your collection.

Above left, a War Tax stamp from Bahrain. Left, a Belgian Railway Parcel stamp and an Italian 'Poste Militaire' (Military Post) stamp.

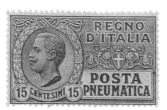

Italian stamps for use on letters carried in pneumatic tubes (left); and a Montserrat stamp (right) overprinted for official use ('On Her Majesty's Service').

AUTOMATIC STAMPS

Some unusual stamps look like the 'stamp' part of a meter mark (a form of postmark, see page 63). These stamps have been introduced by many countries and are produced by electronic vending machines. After inserting money, the purchaser presses a button to select the value of stamp required; the machine then prints the stamp, often on specially-patterned paper. These automatic stamps are sometimes called 'Framas' after the manufacturer of one of the machines that produces them. Another name for them is ATMs, an abbreviation of the German word *Automatenmarken* (meaning 'automatic stamp').

Two Postage Due stamps (above).

POSTAL STATIONERY

As well as adhesive postage stamps, many authorities issue stationery items - postcards, aerogrammes and envelopes - with stamps already printed on them. In addition to the stamps, postal stationery often has attractive pictorial designs which commemorate a special event or feature the country of issue.

Two postal stationery items inspired by philatelic subjects are, above left, a San Marino postcard and, centre, an envelope from Australia. An Austrian aerogramme is shown below.

VALUABLE STAMPS

Of the countless millions of stamps ever issued, there are many stamps that are worth considerable sums of money. This is usually because there are very few of them or because they contain a spectacular error.

Bermuda's first stamp (above). Mauritius 'Post Paid' stamps (right) are similar to the rare 'Post Office' version.

EARLY STAMPS

In 1847 the remote Indian Ocean island of Mauritius became the first British colony to issue a postage stamp. Engraved by Joseph Barnard, a watchmaker in the island's capital of Port Louis, these ld (one penny) and 2d (two penny) stamps bear a crude portrait of Queen Victoria. Instead of the words 'Post Paid', Barnard engraved 'Post Office'. Most of these 'Post Office' Mauritius stamps were used by the Governor's wife, Lady Gomm, on invitations to a Government ball. Only 500 of each value were printed, and very few now exist.

Bermuda's first stamps were produced by its Postmaster, William Perot, in 1848. He used his post-mark canceller to make the stamps, which were sold for a penny each. The stamps were intended for use on letters posted in the mail box after the post office had closed; during opening hours, mail was paid for in cash and these stamps were not used. These 'Perots' were intended for local use only, and therefore very few have survived.

STAMPS ON STAMPS

Most of us are unlikely to own one of the famous rarities mentioned on these pages. However, we can have them in our albums by forming a collection of 'stamps on stamps' - a popular theme. Most of these famous issues, and many others, have appeared on more common stamps. Stamp anniversaries and stamp exhibitions often provide an excuse for depicting them.

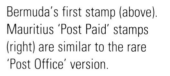

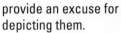

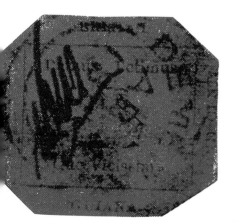

A British Guiana 'cotton-reel'. The stamps were initialled before sale to prevent fraud.

The world's 'rarest stamp' - the unique British Guiana one cent stamp.

This 3 skilling banco stamp from Sweden should be green, not yellow.

This Western Australia stamp has its frame inverted, though it is popularly known as the 'Inverted Swan'.

SCHOOLBOY DISCOVERIES

Perhaps the world's most famous stamp, the British Guiana One Cent black on magenta, was discovered by a schoolboy in British Guiana in 1873. The only one of its kind, this stamp has been described as the 'world's rarest stamp'.

Another valuable stamp from British Guiana is the 'cottonreel' of 1850, so-called because its shape looked like the label at the end of a cottonreel.

One of Europe's rarest stamps is Swedish. Like the British Guiana stamp, it too was discovered by a schoolboy. This stamp, the 3 skilling banco of 1857, is an error of colour, being yellow, the colour of the 8 skilling banco, instead of green. The error was caused by an incorrect part being put into the printing plate when it was made.

The central figure is missing from this Virgin Island stamp: it is called the 'Missing Virgin'.

ERRORS

A similar mistake caused the Cape triangular 'Woodblocks' to be printed in the wrong colours. The 1d was in blue instead of red, and the 4d in red instead of blue. (These locally-produced stamps were called 'Woodblocks' because they looked as if they had been printed from wood engravings.) Other famous errors include the 'Missing Virgin' on the 1867 Virgin Islands 1s stamp, the Western Australia 'Inverted Swan' of 1854 (actually an inverted frame) and the inverted Curtiss 'Jenny' aeroplane on a 1918 US airmail stamp.

Cape of Good Hope 'Woodblocks'. The 4d red stamp is an error, having been printed in the colour of the 1d stamp.

UNUSUAL STAMPS

Most of us think of stamps as being small, rectangular pieces of paper, usually perforated, with a design on one side and gum on the other. This is usually so, but there are many strange exceptions.

SHAPES

The first non-rectangular stamp design, an octagonal one, was issued by Great Britain in 1847 - though the stamps were often cut square from the unperforated sheet. A triangular stamp appeared from the Cape of Good Hope in 1853, and there have been many triangular ones since. Many other shapes have also been used, from diamond to circular. But perhaps the strangest are the 'free-forms' from Sierra Leone and Tonga. These are in many exotic shapes, such as parrots, bananas, water melons, athletes and maps - Norfolk Island, too, has produced map shapes. Many of these issues were self-adhesive. Another strange stamp was produced by Gibraltar in 1969, perforated to the shape of the famous 'Rock'.

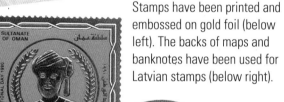

Stamps have been printed and embossed on gold foil (below left). The backs of maps and banknotes have been used for Latvian stamps (below right).

This map-shaped Sierra Leone stamp (left) is on self-adhesive paper, as are the two rectangular ones below.

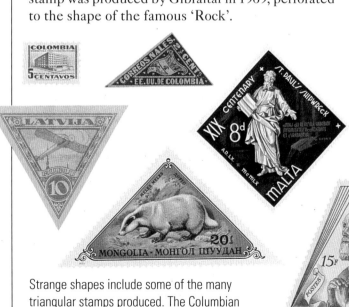

Strange shapes include some of the many triangular stamps produced. The Columbian stamp (top left) is one of the smallest.

Left, a miniature sheet from Paraguay with a record attached to the front. Below is one of a set of stamps from Bhutan that plays folk songs and the national anthem.

PRINTING MATERIALS

Paper is the most common printing surface for a stamp, and lots of different kinds of paper have been used. Many other materials, such as cloth, metal foils, steel, plastic and wood veneer, have been used as well. Stamps have also been printed on the back of old bank notes and maps.

The Himalayan kingdom of Bhutan has issued many unusual stamps, including scented and plastic-moulded ones, and, strangest of all, gramophone record stamps which play the country's national anthem. Paraguay, too, has issued a philatelic gramophone record, though this was stuck to a miniature sheet depicting the band 'Los Paraguayos'.

JOINED AND INVERTED

Stamps of two or more different designs joined together have been issued by many countries. Stamps joined in this way are known as 'se tenant', from the French for 'joined together'. Where the different designs form one picture it is called a composite design.

When one stamp is upside down in relation to another, the stamps are said to be 'tête-bêche' (which, loosely translated from the French, means 'top against bottom'). Such stamps are usually issued by error.

Se tenant stamps. Those from Kiribati have a composite design.

A block of Swiss stamps printed tête-bêche.

THREE DIMENSIONS

The first stamp with a 3-D (three-dimensional) image came from Italy in 1956 to commemorate the United Nations. It depicted a map of the world which, when viewed through special glasses with red and green lenses, appeared to be three-dimensional. Several prismatic-ribbed stamps that provide a 3-D picture have also been issued. In 1988, Austria issued a stamp incorporating a hologram (which gives a 3-D image), and the USA has produced postal stationery envelopes incorporating holograms.

Special spectacles are needed to see the 3-D effect of the Italian stamp above. Holograms (right) require no special aids.

COLLECTING BY COUNTRY

Most collectors probably begin by collecting the stamps of the world. Sooner or later, however, they find that there are far too many stamps for this to be worthwhile, and the collection will need to be limited in some way. The traditional way of doing this is to collect the stamps of just one or two countries. This still gives lots to collect.

CHOOSING A COUNTRY

Which country should you choose? Most people find that collecting the stamps of the country where they live is best. There are many reasons for this. It is usually easy to find out about them, and new issues can be obtained easily from a post office. Also, because they are popular, earlier stamps are more likely to be found at a stamp dealer, or be available to swap with a fellow collector.

Other countries might be chosen because you already have a lot of stamps from them, or because you have friends or relatives there that can keep you supplied with stamps. Maybe you find a particular country's stamps attractive because of their designs or the way they are printed.

GREAT BRITAIN
25 April 1975
European Architectural Heritage Year

11th June 1975
Sailing

UNITED STATES
Great Americans

CANCELLATIONS

Stamps may be collected used or unused; but they should always be in good condition. Do not include damaged or heavily-postmarked stamps in your collection, because they will spoil its appearance. However, used stamps with suitable postmarks are often quite difficult to find. Shown here are some used stamps which have different grades of cancellation.

  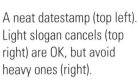  

A neat datestamp (top left). Light slogan cancels (top right) are OK, but avoid heavy ones (right).

The Christmas slogan (above) and postmark (right) obscure the design.

Pages from straightforward Great Britain and USA collections (left). Their blank pages allow for flexibility in the layout. The Australian collection below is mounted on pre-printed pages, which allows less scope for expansion.

AUSTRALIA

2 – 16th October. Tenth International Congress of Account-, Sydney. Designed by G. Andrews; printed by the Reserve < of Australia. No watermark. 13 x 13½.

2 – 15th November. Pioneer Life. Designed by R. Ingpen; ted by the Reserve Bank of Australia. No watermark. 13½ x 13 (5c, 10c, 60c), 13 x 13½ (others).

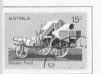 

2 – 29th November. Christmas. Designs adapted by W. Tamlyn) and L. Stirling (35c); printed by the Reserve Bank of Australia. watermark. f 13 x 13½.

LOOKING AHEAD

Before you begin to collect a country's stamps seriously, it is a good idea to see what is involved by taking a look through a stamp catalogue. Many countries have issued so many stamps that you might never hope to obtain them all; others' might be so expensive that you could never afford them. For example, Britain has issued over 1,500 stamps in total, including 70 in 1991; France 3,000 (60 in 1991); the USA 2,500 (80 in 1991) and Germany (West and Berlin) about 2,000 (90 in 1991). In such cases it might be a good idea to limit the scope of the collection. You could collect stamps of a particular monarch's reign or from a particular period - German stamps since reunification, or those of a country since its independence, are examples. You could even collect the stamps of a single issue: there are many sets that lend themselves to this. Long-running definitive sets in particular give plenty of scope for study, with different printings, varieties, booklet panes and other items to form a highly-specialized collection.

Choosing a less popular country or one that no longer issues stamps may seem a good idea. But it may be difficult to obtain sufficient stamps to keep you interested in your collection.

COLLECTOR'S HINT
It is best not to mix used and unused stamps in the same set. Instead, display them as separate sets, either on the same page, below one another, or on a new sheet.

DEVELOPING THE COLLECTION

Just as some countries issue too many stamps to collect, others may not issue enough to keep you busy or you may have collected most of the stamps. Instead of starting another collection, an interesting way of developing your collection is to extend it beyond the scope of the catalogue. This can involve the careful study of your stamps to find varieties and errors, and the addition of stamp booklets and postal stationery or, perhaps, 'Cinderellas' (see page 66).

POSTAL HISTORY

The collection could be extended backwards to show the history of your chosen country's postal service. This may include items carried before stamps were introduced, or perhaps letters using another country's stamps. Stamps on cover could be collected to show some special use, such as registration or airmail, or they could simply demonstrate different postal rates in use.

Today, much mail is sorted by machine. Often the envelopes bear markings that show this aspect of the post. Many modern special postal services do not use stamps at all: look on the envelopes of business mail and 'junk' mail, for example. Such material is often thrown away, yet it is nevertheless part of a country's postal history. A few pages of such material can expand the interest and scope of your collection.

POSTMARKS

Postmarks provide another means of extending your collection. They may show some unusual aspect of the post, such as mail sorted on a railway travelling post office or posted from a ship at sea. If you collect the stamps from a small country, it might be possible to obtain postmarks from every post office. If a larger country is your subject, a range of the postmarks used there may be of interest. With imagination and study, even a small-country collection can be developed.

Covers can reveal many aspects of postal services in operation. Shown top to bottom are a British cover posted without a stamp and with postage due markings and label; an underpaid cover from the USA with American and British markings; a Belgian Express letter; and a triangular postmark usually used on mail containing advertising leaflets.

1955-58
DEFINITIVE ISSUE

Watermark St. Edward's Crown.
Watermark sideways ex coils
Varieties

white flaw
over "O"
Coil 2

dot between rose
& thistle at right
Coil 10

retouched "2" leaving "d"
nearer to "2" and fatter
Coil T(5)

extra leg to "R"
of "REVENUE"
Coil T(2)

A page from a specialized collection of British definitives. The enlarged
illustrations point out constant flaws found on the stamps, and neatly-typed
notes give further details. The stamps are mounted in protective strips.

COLLECTOR'S HINT
Covers and stationery items
can often be overlapped
to display only the
relevant parts, thus taking
up less space in
the album.

COLLECTING BY THEME

$1.10 CAICOS ISLANDS

Christmas 1984

PINOCCHIO, JIMINY CRICKET & FIGARO

SANTA CLAUS IS COMING TO TOWN

The Tale of Peter Rabbit
The Year of the Child

9p

Thematic collecting (which is also known as topical collecting, especially in the USA) is an increasingly popular way of forming a stamp collection. Unlike traditional collecting, where the object is to obtain all the stamps of a particular country or period, the thematic collector chooses stamps by what they depict. A thematic collection is likely to contain old and new stamps from many different countries, and it need not contain every stamp that might fit the chosen theme in order to appear 'complete'. Thus a really interesting and unusual collection can be made without great expense.

Tom Sawyer

United States 8c

PENRHYN
NORTHERN COOK ISLANDS
95¢

CHOOSING A THEME

The choice of theme is huge. Stamps have been issued for just about every subject you can think of. Some themes have large numbers of stamps devoted to them and are extremely popular - such as birds (over 7,500 stamps), mammals (5,000), ships (11,000) and railways (6,000). You can also collect by theme on a small scale - a more manageable number might be 650 for a collection of stamps showing fungi. Perhaps small themes could be a sideline or 'fun' collection in addition to your main collection.

Above are four stamps showing storybook characters - just one of the many hundreds of themes you can choose to collect.

Eclectus Parrot

Tristan da Cunha

ROCKHOPPER PENGUIN

E II R

SAMOA 50

Eudyptes chrysocome moseleyi

Mindre hackspett
Dendrocopos minor

Sverige 240

Wildlife subjects are very popular. There are thousands of bird stamps (above), but less of subjects such as reptiles.

НР БЪЛГАРИЯ
поща ст 32
Локомотив - 1943
100 Български държавни железници
1988

DAS SOZIALISTISCHE EISENBAHN-WESEN UND SEINE TRADITIONEN

DDR

AUSTRALIA 20c
Double Fairlie, Western Australia

Another popular theme offering scope for development is railways. Around 6,000 stamps depicting locomotives and related subjects have been issued.

Richard Trevithick 1803 r

50 GR POLSKA

High-Speed Train 12p

1975 British Rail Inter-City Service HST

Locomotive 1870s
USA 2c

A PARTICULAR INTEREST

You will obviously choose your subject because it has some interest for you. Perhaps you are keen on sport or animals. Although you will probably begin by trying to collect all the sport or animal stamps that you can, you will soon find that such a task is too great. Instead, why not break the subject down further? Try collecting stamps showing a particular sport, such as football, cricket or tennis, or stamps depicting an animal species - the choice is endless.

You will probably find that collecting in this way is much more interesting.

In many ways, collecting by theme is much more challenging than collecting by country. You will need to search through stamp catalogues to see which stamps fit your chosen theme. And you will certainly need to find out about the subject you have chosen in order to tell an organized story when the stamps are mounted in your album.

A page from a collection on the theme of cats. Simple captions explain the stamps. There are many catalogues and checklists available to help you build thematic collections.

CATS

A cartoon cat

Tabby Siamese

A lucky cat

Tabby

Cat with wool

Siamese

Cat with kitten

Cat with mouse

Kitten

$7.50

1603

Illustrated Cat Stamp Checklist

Part 1 Domestic Cats 1930-1988

COLLECTOR'S HINT
Always remember that a thematic collection is a stamp collection. Be very sparing in the use of things other than philatelic items, such as photographs.

Charles Dickens was born in Portsmouth on 7 February 1812. His early life was spent in hardship, experiences reflected in DAVID COPPERFIELD. He began his writing career as a reporter, his early works, such as PICKWICK PAPERS, being published in serial form. In 1853 he began charity readings of his works. A tour to America in 1867 undermined his failing health and he died, aged 58, on 9 June 1870 at Gads Hill, Kent. He wrote 16 novels.

SCENES FROM THE NOVELS

A STORY IN STAMPS

Thematic stamp collecting can be as simple as just obtaining stamps showing a particular subject. It can be more challenging, too, particularly if the stamps are used to illustrate the development of a story or an idea. For example, instead of forming a haphazard collection of stamps issued for the Olympic Games, the history and growth of the Olympic Games could be told through the stamps. Such a collection might begin with the Games' origins in ancient Greece, show their development, the ceremonies that took place, the buildings at the Olympic site, as well as the various sports that were contested. It might then move on to the modern Games, show why they were reintroduced, their gradual development and the cities that have hosted them, the people who helped organize them, famous athletes, the introduction of the Winter Games, and so on. In order to tell its story well, a collection like this would probably contain many postal items that have not been issued to commemorate the Games themselves.

There are two types of elephant:
African and Indian

Elephants can be seen on safari. In the east, elephants are
used as working animals and on ceremonial occasions

Elephants can be seen in zoos
and at the circus

FIRST DAY COVER

"RAJA" TUSKER OF SRI DALADA MALIGAWA

Shown are pages from three thematic collections. Note the different styles and amounts of information included on the pages. A stamp booklet and first day cover have been used in the elephant collection.

CAREFUL RESEARCH

In order to develop a story or idea through stamps, you will need to research your subject well. Only when you understand the subject will you be able to see how seemingly unconnected stamps will fit into the collection. You will need to write some notes linking your stamps together on the album page, and developing the story you are telling. This will help make sense of your collection when you show it to other people. Such a collection may be more difficult to form, but it will also be much more rewarding.

PLANNING

To form any thematic collection, you need to have some sort of plan in mind. A collection of 'animals' could simply be divided into types of animal from aardvark to zebra. One on 'The Horse' would need much more careful thought. For example, it might show the different breeds and their uses in farming, transport, sport and so on. Before you start collecting, write out a brief plan showing the way you intend to develop your theme. It will help you to see how and where a particular stamp will fit in.

VARIATIONS ON A THEME

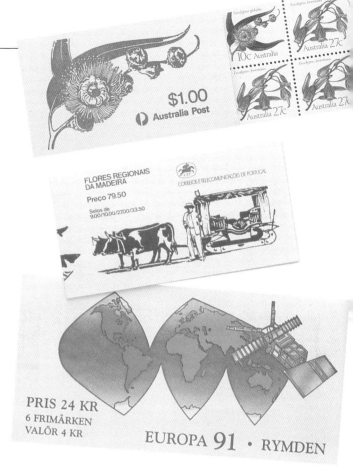

A thematic collection need not be devoted just to stamps. The addition of other philatelic material that helps to tell your story, such as postmarks and postal stationery, can give your collection much more variety.

POSTMARKS

Stamps in a thematic collection are generally best collected unused so that the designs are clear. However, postmarks can play an important part in their own right. There are many pictorial postmarks that will fit into a theme. These may depict a subject relevant to the collection - a person or building, for example - or may commemorate an event that fits the story. Meter marks (see page 63) and postmarks with advertising slogans on them can fit in, too. If they also cancel a stamp that is part of the theme, so much the better. Postmarks should be clear and easily read.

Below are special event and slogan postmarks useful for a ships collection (left), and two air-related meter marks.

These stamp booklet covers will fit thematic collections of flowers, animals, transport, space and maps.

DISPLAYING POSTMARKS

If the complete envelope is not needed, then the postmark and stamp can be cut out neatly and mounted on the page. On the other hand, you might want to keep the envelope complete, but do not want to take up too much room on the album page. Therefore, cut a rectangular hole in the page, and mount the envelope behind it. The stamp and the postmark will show through the hole.

STATIONERY

Postal stationery items - postcards, envelopes and aerogrammes - are issued by many countries. The printed stamps on these items often have a suitable design that will fit a thematic collection, and many also have other pictorial elements which can be useful. Australia often issues pre-stamped envelopes to commemorate subjects not thought important enough for a stamp. The USA and Italy also issue many pictorial stationery items, and aerogrammes are produced by countries throughout the world. Stamp booklets often have pictorial covers, and so should not be overlooked. 'Cinderella' items (explained on page 66) can also be included.

STAMP DETAILS

Take a close look at your stamps, because just a tiny part of a design will often be found to fit a theme. Look out, too, for watermarks. These often overlooked parts of a stamp can provide some surprises: some stamps from Tonga, for example, have a 'tortoise' watermark that perhaps could fit an 'animal' collection.

Overprints can be a source of designs, and labels found attached to some stamps may also be useful. Varieties and errors can add interest to any collection - a thematic one is no exception.

Tongan tortoise watermark.

Flower overprint.

Advert attached to Italian stamp.

Items of postal stationery - pre-stamped aerogrammes (above), envelopes (centre) and postcards (right) - often have interesting and colourful designs which will fit into a thematic collection.

HOW STAMPS ARE MADE

It is a complex process from an original idea to issuing a finished stamp. From the hundreds of suggestions for stamp issues made each year - by individuals, or organizations wanting to commemorate an event - the postal administration has to select just a few to make an interesting issuing programme. It may take two or three years before a stamp is finally put on sale.

THE ARTIST

Having decided on the need for a stamp issue, a postal administration will ask one or more artists to produce suitable designs. The artists will set to work, researching the subject in order to make sure that the design is correct. When the research is complete, artwork, in the form of a drawing, painting or photograph, will be presented for consideration by the postal administration. This presentation will include the proposed lettering and other design elements. When a design has been selected, any alterations that are needed are carried out. The finished artwork is usually prepared at a much larger size than the printed stamp. Once the postal administration has approved it, this artwork is then sent to the printer.

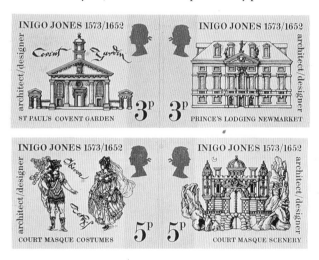

PERFORATION AND ROULETTE

The first stamps were cut from the printed sheet with scissors. The use of perforated sheets, which have rows of tiny holes punched between the stamps, makes it easier to separate them neatly.

Sheets that are perforated row by row, first in one direction and then the other, are described as 'line perforated'. Stamps perforated in this way often have corners that are uneven, because the perforation holes do not coincide. This unevenness is particularly noticeable on blocks of stamps.

A 'comb perforator' - so called because it looks like a comb - perforates the top and sides of a stamp in one operation. It moves down the sheet, one row of stamps at a time, in one direction only. The holes where the lines cross over at the corners of the stamps are usually even and regular.

AT THE PRINTER

What happens next will depend on the printing process used. If the stamp is to be printed by the intaglio method, a skilled engraver will engrave the design, in reverse, onto a block of metal. During this work, proofs, which are test printings, will be taken to check its progress.

The finished die will be hardened and the image transferred, under pressure, to a transfer roller; the design now appears the right way round. This roller is in turn hardened and used to place the design, again in reverse, on the printing plate, once for each stamp in the sheet. Colour proofs (test printings) may be taken from the die in order to choose a suitable colour for the issued stamp.

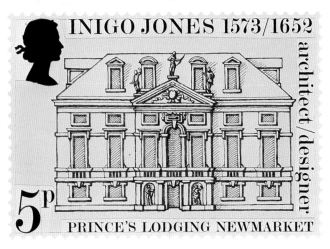

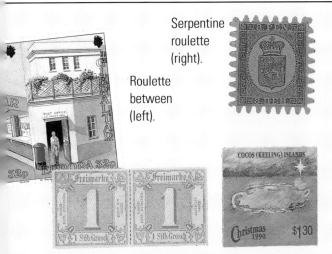

Another means of separating stamps is rouletting. The paper is cut or pierced but, unlike perforation, no paper is removed. There are many types of roulette pattern - arcs, crosses, diamonds, lozenge, pin, sawtooth, serpentine and zigzag are names for some of them.

PHOTOCHEMICAL PROCESSES

When a stamp is printed by the photogravure or litho method, a photochemical process is used to transfer the stamp design the required number of times to a printing cylinder or plate. If the stamp is to be printed in more than one colour, a separate plate will be needed for each. When the printing plates are put onto a printing press, proofs are made. These proofs will be checked and, if necessary, the colours will be adjusted. When the presses are correctly adjusted, the stamps will be produced.

Most multicoloured stamps are printed from just four colours: yellow, cyan (blue), magenta (red) and black. However, most multicoloured British stamps printed by the photogravure method (see next page) use many more different coloured inks to achieve their effect. By using a magnifying glass you can see the tiny dots of ink that make up the stamp's picture.

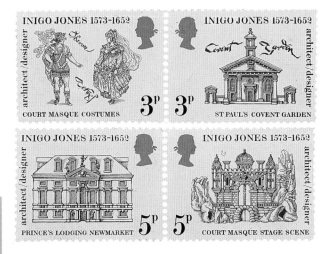

Stamp-size essays (far left); the original artwork; the final redrawn artwork before the colours, values and pairings have been finalized; and, above, the issued stamps.

PRINTING

Stamps may be printed in sheets, or in a continuous roll which is then cut into single sheets. The sheets will be perforated either as part of the printing process or in a separate operation. The finished sheets are checked for errors, counted and finally distributed to post offices for use.

PRINTING STAMPS

There are four main methods used for printing stamps. Sometimes two of these, usually intaglio and either photogravure or lithography, are combined in one stamp. This enables an engraved design (which collectors consider is the best method for printing stamps, but which cannot be used to produce a multicoloured design) to be given added colour.

Embossing has been used in stamp printing since the 1840s. The paper is placed between two dies, one having the image (design) in relief (raised) and the other with it in recess (sunk). The two dies are brought together and the image is impressed in the paper, giving a raised design.

INTAGLIO

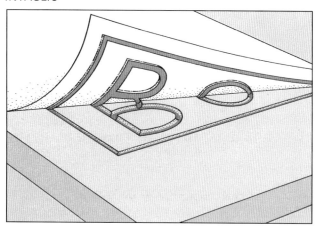

This printing method, also known to philatelists as line engraving or recess printing, was used to print the Penny Black. The design is cut into the printing surface. This is then inked and wiped, leaving the ink in the cut lines. Paper is laid on the printing surface, under pressure, and thus picks up the ink of the design. The printed design can usually be felt as a slightly raised surface.

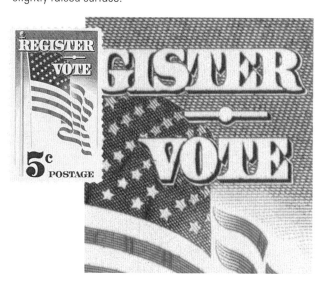

PHOTOGRAVURE

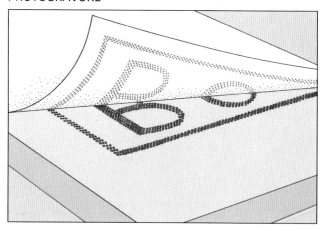

A modern variation of intaglio is photogravure. With this method, a photographic negative of the stamp design is broken into a screen of small dots and etched onto a copper cylinder. Each 'dot' of the design forms a tiny cell in the cylinder, and varies in depth. When printing, the cylinder is inked and wiped, leaving ink in the cells: the shallow cells hold less ink, giving a light tone, the deeper cells hold more and therefore give a darker tone. Look through a magnifying glass to see the tiny dots that form a photogravure stamp's design. The dots are particularly noticeable along the edges of letters and figures, which will appear ragged.

OTHER PRINTING METHODS

Photography has rarely been used to print stamps, though it is used in the production process, to make printing plates. The most famous photographically-printed stamps are those made during the Siege of Mafeking in 1900. The 3d value depicts Colonel Baden Powell, the founder of the Scout movement.

Stamps have also been produced using a typewriter - this one is from Long Island. Typewriters have also been used to over-print and surcharge stamps.

LETTERPRESS

Also called surface printing or typography, letterpress is the opposite of intaglio. The design is engraved, but the areas *not* required to print are removed from the printing surface. Ink is applied to the raised surface of the design, and this is transferred to the paper. Stamps printed directly from printers' metal type are printed by this method. The pressure applied when printing sometimes leaves a slightly raised impression of the design on the back of the stamp, and the ink can squeeze slightly over the edges of the design. This, too, can be seen with a magnifying glass.

LITHOGRAPHY

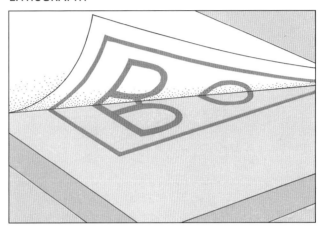

Common in modern stamp printing, lithography uses the fact that oil and water do not mix. A special greasy ink is used to transfer the stamp design to a printing surface, which is then moistened and ink applied. The ink sticks to the greasy portion of the printing surface, which is then impressed onto the paper. In a variation of this method known as offset litho, the inked image is first impressed onto a rubber 'blanket' which prints it onto the paper. Like photogravure stamps, many litho stamps have a 'screen' of dots. However, with lithography they are clearer, and lettering viewed under a magnifying glass will be seen to have neat edges.

FORGERIES AND FAKES

Many stamps are worth considerable amounts of money. It is not surprising, therefore, to find that a large number have been forged or tampered with in an attempt to deceive and defraud collectors. Sometimes, attempts are made to forge a genuine stamp's overprint or postmark.

The Star of David on the crown, and the hammer and sickle forming the 1'D', reveal this German propaganda forgery (above left). The Jersey occupation stamps (right) are not forgeries, but can you spot the 'GR' and 'V' (for Victory) in the scrolling?

FAMOUS FORGERS

Two famous forgers were Francois Fournier and Jean de Sperati. Fournier, active at the turn of the century, offered his forgeries, which he regarded as 'works of art', to collectors unable to afford the originals. Sperati produced his work between the two world wars, forging over 500 different valuable stamps. Today, reference collections of both men's work exist, enabling experts to identify items forged by them.

In the 1870s a forged British 1s stamp was used on telegraph forms at the London Stock Exchange (left). Many years later the forgery was discovered by a stamp dealer who noticed that on some stamps the corner check letters had combinations not used on genuine stamps (shown at bottom). The culprit was never caught.

Jean de Sperati, the forger of many valuable stamps.

DEFRAUDING THE AUTHORITIES

Not all forgeries are intended to deceive collectors. Many are meant to defraud the postal authorities. They have also been produced by enemy countries during a war. For example, German propaganda forgeries made during World War 2 based their designs on current British stamps, but with subtle alterations intended to discredit Britain.

Forgery still continues today, usually to defraud postal authorities. For example, in April 1991, the *Times* of India reported that five men, three of them postal staff, had been arrested for preparing and selling forged aerogrammes, resulting in a huge loss to the Indian post office.

SECURITY MEASURES

Stamp-issuing authorities often make great efforts to prevent stamps from being forged. An engraved and easily-recognizable portrait of Queen Victoria was used for the Penny Black because it was considered to be more difficult to forge. The machine-engraved background made the design even more complex.

A watermark is another important security device. Fluorescent security markings, visible in ultraviolet light, have been used on stamps from the Cook Islands, Ecuador and Hong Kong.

The removal of postmarks is another security problem. To try to prevent this, fugitive inks, which run when immersed in water, and varnish coatings, have been used.

FAKES AND FACSIMILES

Genuine stamps which have been altered in some way are known as fakes. A used stamp may have the postmark removed and be re-gummed to make it appear unused. Colours may be changed or perforations added or removed. Damaged stamps that have been repaired are also fakes.

Facsimiles are stamps that have been copied from originals and are offered for sale as such. They are often marked in some way to make it clear that they are not real stamps. However, if the marking should be removed, they can be difficult to tell apart from genuine stamps.

The vertical lines between 'Postes' and the central oval give away these Suez Canal company forgeries (right): on the genuine stamps they are cross-hatched.

The coloured bar security device at the bottom of this stamp makes it hard to copy.

This Queensland stamp has been used for revenue purposes (see page 67). Attempts have been made to remove its pen cancellation.

This Gibraltar stamp is not the forgery it appears to be: in fact it has been cut from postal stationery and given a crude perforation.

A copy with false postmark (left) of the valuable 1857 6d stamp from Western Australia.

Copies of two rare stamps (right) - the 1d 'Post Office' Mauritius and the 2c rose 'cottonreel' of British Guiana.

Forged Irish £1 stamps were used to defraud the Post Office. The forged stamp (top) has line perforations (see page 46), the genuine stamp (bottom) is comb perforated.

EXPERT COMMITTEES

Detecting forgeries and fakes can be difficult. To help collectors, many large philatelic societies and some dealers offer an 'expertising' service. For a fee, they will examine an item and assess how genuine they believe it to be. This assessment is recorded on a certificate, which can be kept with the stamp.

MISTAKES

Two stamps with inverted centres (above and right).

A colour has been missed off this se tenant block of bird stamps (below).

Stamps which have errors caused during the printing process are very popular with collectors. Many with missing colours or inverted centres, for example, are quite striking and much sought after. These, and other major errors, such as incorrectly perforated stamps, and those printed in the wrong colour or on the wrong paper, are often of great value.

00094

The arrowed stamp (left) has a constant flaw. And something on the printing surface has caused the 'missing corner' on the bottom stamp.

This mirror image (above right) has been caused by stacking a sheet on still-wet stamps.

PRINTING FLAWS

There are many minor flaws which can be found on stamps. While not making the stamp very valuable, they will add variety to any collection. For example, damage caused to the printing surface at some stage during its manufacture will often be so small that it goes unnoticed by the printer. Keen-eyed collectors soon spot these flaws, however!

Sometimes, after the stamps have been printed and issued, the printer attempts to correct a flaw.

This is very hard to do, and the correction is often detectable. Therefore, subsequent printings of the stamp will show the flaw 'retouched' (corrected), providing a further item of interest to the collector.

When a flaw occurs on every sheet of stamps printed from a plate, it is said to be 'constant'. Flaws that last for only part of the printing run, perhaps because something sticks to the printing surface and is later removed, are called 'inconstant'.

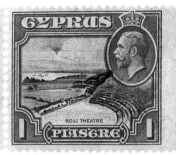

The perforations are missing between the two stamps above. Imperforate errors should be collected in pairs.

A flaw on these Hungarian stamps (right) has given one of them a face value of 1.78.

DESIGN ERRORS

Another type of mistake that can be found on stamps is that made by the artist. This could be a simple spelling mistake, an incorrect inscription, or something wrong in the stamp's design. For example, stamps issued by St Kitts in 1903 showed Columbus looking through a telescope, although telescopes had not been invented in Columbus's time. Sometimes, after such a mistake has been spotted, the stamp is reissued with a corrected design.

A design error: the aeroplane on the left has no tail fin - it would be unlikely to fly!

Columbus uses a telescope before it was invented!

Governor Phillip meeting the Home Society
NORFOLK ISLAND

Above, the French philosopher Descartes and his work 'Discours de la Méthode'; the stamp on the right is incorrectly inscribed 'Discours sur la Méthode'. Left, Governor Phillip meets the 'Home Society'. The design was also issued with the correct 'Home Secretary' caption.

Governor Phillip meeting the Home Secretary
NORFOLK ISLAND

COLLECTOR'S HINT
A small drawing showing an enlarged detail of the stamp, or a paper arrow (stuck to the album page, not the stamp), can help point out difficult-to-see flaws.

EARLY POSTAL SYSTEMS

Although the world's first adhesive postage stamp, the Penny Black, came into use just over 150 years ago, postal services had been in existence for many hundreds of years before then. There are references to postal services in the Bible. And dating from even earlier (around 3000-2000 BC) are letters on baked clay tablets that have been found in Cappadocia (in modern Turkey). These letters even had their own clay envelopes!

A MESSAGE RELAYED

Messenger services of some sort were necessary to most ancient civilizations, and were usually organized by the king or by merchants. The first relay postal system is thought to have been founded by King Cyrus, ruler of the Persian Empire, in 539 BC. Stables were set up a day's journey apart, and riders travelling by day and night carried messages between them in relays. In the Roman Empire, the building of an excellent road network and the well-organized government messenger service, the *Cursus Publicus*, were essential to the administration of the Empire. The *Cursus Publicus* used horse-drawn coaches as well as just horses for transport.

Little is known of postal services in Europe after the fall of the Roman Empire, but by the Middle Ages, many different systems were in operation, run by merchants, universities, monasteries, kings and princes, and by large towns and cities. The late Middle Ages saw the rise of an international service run by the Counts of Thurn and Taxis. It eventually covered most of Europe and lasted until 1867.

A clay letter written in about 2000 BC. The letter still has its protective envelope.

The world's first adhesive postage stamp, the Penny Black (above), was issued in 1840. It depicted a young Queen Victoria.

A postal carriage of the *Cursus Publicus* depicted on a stone relief carving. The *Cursus Publicus* carried mail throughout the Roman Empire.

THE FIRST MODERN SYSTEM

In England, the first 'Master of the Postes', Sir Brian Tuke, was appointed by King Henry VIII in 1516. Private mail services were discouraged, and after 1591 all mail had to be carried by the royal postal system. The General Letter Office, forerunner of the General Post Office (GPO), was established in 1660 under King Charles II, who appointed Henry Bishop as Postmaster General. Bishop was responsible for the introduction of a postmark showing the day and month of posting.

The British postal system was well-organised but expensive. Letters were charged by the number of sheets and the distance they travelled. In the 1830s, Rowland Hill began a campaign to reform the postal service, and in 1839 letters were charged by weight and not distance travelled, thus bringing down the cost of postage. On 6 May 1840 the Penny Black came into use, along with pre-stamped envelopes and wrappers (known as 'Mulreadys' after their designer, William Mulready). These items meant that the pre-payment of postage was now easy.

Special postal stationery was issued at the same time as the Penny Black, to pre-pay postage. The design, by William Mulready, was ridiculed by the public and soon withdrawn.

FROM CLAY TO MAILCOACH

Many aspects of early postal systems, from clay tablets to mailcoaches, have been illustrated on stamps. They can make an interesting collection about postal history.

A letter on a stone tablet.

A Roman post cart used in Gaul (France).

The Counts of Thurn and Taxis (above) ran an international service.

A Roman courier on horseback.

A 14th-16th century Russian messenger.

A German messenger from Nuremberg, about 1700.

An Irish 'Bianconi' mailcoach with outside passengers.

AIRMAIL

Although the first successful aeroplane - the Wright Brothers' 'Flyer' - took to the skies in 1903, mail had been carried by air long before then. In fact, pigeons were the first means of carrying mail by air: they were used by the Romans to carry messages.

PIGEONS AND BALLOONS

A more recent use of pigeons was during the Siege of Paris (1870-71), when photographically-reduced messages were flown into the city by pigeons that had been smuggled out by balloon. The balloons, too, were used to fly mail out of the city - but because they were not steerable, they could fly only when weather conditions were favourable. Items flown from Paris during the siege are much sought after by collectors.

Later, motor-powered and steerable 'dirigible' balloons were built. The most famous of these were the German Zeppelins, which made possible the regular carriage of mail by balloon. From the late 1920s, Zeppelins made many well-publicized flights around the world. Mail carried on these flights often bears colourful hand-stamps detailing the journey.

A copy of the journal *Gazette des Absents* flown from Paris by balloon during the siege of 1870-71.

The German Zeppelin airships (above and left) introduced regular airmail services. The cover (below) was carried on an aeroplane launched by catapult in mid-Atlantic from the French ship *Isle de France* (see page 59).

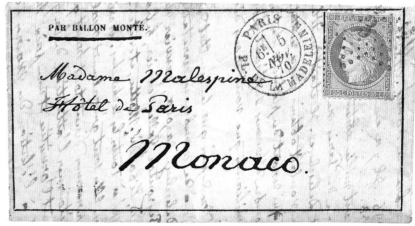

AEROPLANES

Meanwhile, the early aeroplanes had begun to carry mail. During these early years, mail was often carried at aviation meetings for publicity purposes and as a souvenir of the event. Of course, as the aeroplane developed, so did airmail routes. Mail was often flown on pioneering flights, and special stamps were sometimes provided for the journeys. For example, Newfoundland issued several stamps for early trans-Atlantic flights.

A card from the world's first official airmail flight (top); a Newfoundland airmail cover (right); an overprint for the first trans-Atlantic airpost in 1919 (far right); an Italian aerogramme depicting the 50th anniversary of a 1940 trans-Atlantic flight (below); and a modern first flight cover (bottom).

The world's first official airmail was carried between Allahabad and Naini in India in 1911. Britain's first official airmail, between Windsor and London, also took place in 1911, as did that of the USA. In 1918 the US Post Office took over the Aerial Mail Service: during the next seven years it flew over 20 million kilometres and carried 300 million letters.

In these first years, airmail services could not be taken for granted: many pilots were killed while flying their low-performance aircraft across the world. Nevertheless, the demand for quick and regular air communications proved a spur to developing the better and more reliable aircraft that entered service in the 1930s.

AIRMAIL TODAY

New airmail services are still being introduced today. Usually, the first flight on a new airmail route is commemorated by a souvenir cover, and often by a special postmark, too. These first-flight covers can be used in a collection to show the development of airmail routes around the world.

malaysia AIRLINES

FIRST FLIGHT

KUALA LUMPUR BRISBANE

Queensland's Great Barrier Reef.

PENERBANGAN PERTAMA
31 OKTOBER 1990

Area Manager
Malaysia Airlines
80 Albert Street (17th Floor)
Brisbane
Queensland 4000
AUSTRALIA

UNUSUAL POSTAL SERVICES

Most of us take for granted the ease with which we can buy a stamp and put our mail into a box for delivery by the postman on his daily round. Yet in many remote and inaccessible places it is not so easy to receive and send mail.

BY LAND...

Most forms of transport - from travelling on foot to the sophisticated vehicles of today's postal authorities - have been used to carry mail by land. Many of the unusual ones have employed animals. For example, between 1846 and 1904 a service using bullock-drawn carts operated in India. Reindeer have drawn mail sledges over the inhospitable terrain of Scandinavia and Russia, dogs have been used in England and Alaska, and cats in Belgium! And camels have been employed not only in Africa and the Middle East, where you might expect to see them, but also in Australia and the USA during the 19th century.

Letters sealed in zinc containers were floated down the River Seine during the siege of Paris (right).

Throwing letters in bottles in to the sea (left) does not guarantee delivery!

This Botswana stamp depicts the carrying of mail in Africa by the Mafeking to Gubulawayo Runner Post (above).

Carrying mail by foot. This Maori (New Zealand) postman (above) is carrying the mail in a plaited bag.

A 17th century hand-drawn sled and a later horse-drawn sleigh were used to convey mail over Russia's icy wastes (above left). In contrast, camels have carried mail across the world's deserts.

Mail in India was transported by bullock-drawn carts (left). The famous Pony Express (below) carried mail across the rugged country of the western USA.

WATER...

War often prevents mail from being delivered. When Paris was besieged by the Prussians in 1870-71, mail was flown out of the city by balloon - and some mail intended for the city was placed in watertight zinc balls known as 'boules de Moulins' and floated down the River Seine!

Equally resourceful were the inhabitants of the remote Scottish island of St Kilda. They sealed letters in hollowed-out driftwood attached to an inflated sheep's bladder. These packages were then cast adrift in the North Atlantic, where current and wind, with luck, carried them to shore on the mainland. This mail system continued in use until the island was evacuated in 1930.

Similarly, mail from the Pacific island of Niuafo'ou, Tonga, was sealed in a tin box and swum out to the waiting mail ship. Colourful 'Tin Can Mail' markings can be found on letters carried by this unusual system.

... AND AIR

Carrying mail by air is probably the fastest and most direct method, and just about every form of flight has been used, from pigeon to jet. At first, flying mail long distances over water was fraught with danger.

In the 1920s and 1930s, therefore, experiments were made to catapult mail-carrying aircraft from ships in mid-Atlantic, thus speeding delivery. The first successful flight was made from the French ship *Isle de France* in 1928. Later, the small seaplane *Mercury* was carried into the air by the larger *Maia*. The faster *Mercury* was then launched from *Maia* to deliver the mail more quickly!

Carried piggy-back fashion, the mail-carrying flying-boat was launched from a larger flying-boat in mid air.

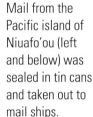

Mail from the Pacific island of Niuafo'ou (left and below) was sealed in tin cans and taken out to mail ships.

Catapult-launched aeroplanes were used to shorten delivery times across the Atlantic. Here (above) a plane is launched from the German ship *Westfalen*.

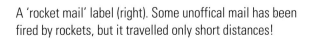

A 'rocket mail' label (right). Some unoffical mail has been fired by rockets, but it travelled only short distances!

FIRST DAY COVERS

A first day cover is an envelope bearing a stamp postmarked on the first day that the stamp could be used. (The first ever first day cover would be one bearing a Penny Black cancelled on 6 May 1840.)

Collecting first day covers is now a popular part of stamp collecting. Envelopes specially printed with a design relevant to the stamp issue are produced by post offices and private manufacturers. These covers often contain a stiffener card that provides information about the stamp issue. Special post-marks with pictorial designs are also produced to cancel the stamps - and popular stamp issues, such as those connected with royal families, often attract several different designs relating to the event.

Similar to first day covers in appearance are those produced to mark a special event, the difference being that the stamps are not always cancelled on the first day of their issue.

Another item related to the first day cover is the maximum card (Maxicard). This is a picture postcard, the design of which is connected to that of the stamp. The stamp is stuck on the picture side of the card and cancelled with an appropriate postmark.

All these items can be bought from stamp dealers, but many collectors like to make their own. For example, the British Post Office publishes a fortnightly *Postmark Bulletin** which lists the special postmarks it produces and tells you where and how to obtain them.

*Subscription details from: British Philatelic Bureau, 20 Brandon Street, Edinburgh, EH3 5TT.

DISPLAYING COVERS

Special albums are available for storing a collection of covers or cards. These contain pages of transparent pockets, one or two to a page, into which the covers are slipped. The pockets usually contain a thin card,

A selection of first day covers with, top, a special event cover and, bottom left, a Maxicard.

and the covers are mounted, using transparent photo corners, on either side - thus each pocket will hold two covers. Pockets are available with an opening at the side or the top; the top-opening type is preferable because it will not let a loose cover fall into the album's binding mechanism.

PREPARING FIRST DAY COVERS

When preparing first day covers, don't stick the stamps too near the envelope's edge, and ensure they are straight and neat. The postmark will be seen easily if you place the stamps in a row across the top of the envelope rather than in a block.

When sticking the stamps down, make sure you leave enough room for the address. A typewritten address looks much neater than one written by hand; better still are small pre-printed self-adhesive address labels.

Special albums with clear plastic pockets are available to protect your covers and cards.

POSTMARKS

Any mark applied to an item sent through the post during the course of its journey is a postmark. Such marks may be handwritten, or applied by hand-stamp or machine. They may show the type of service paid for, how the item was sent, the route taken, the time and place of posting, charges to be paid, or other special instructions. The best known type of postmark gives the time and place of posting.

EARLY POSTMARKS

Postmarks reveal the history and development of the postal service. The earliest British date-stamp was devised by Henry Bishop in 1661. It showed the day and month of posting and was introduced to answer complaints about delays in the post. In 1680 William Dockwra's London Penny Post used a triangular mark showing that postage had been paid.

There are some postmarks that prevent a stamp being re-used. They are known as cancellations. The first of them was the so-called 'Maltese Cross' used on the Penny Black in 1840. It gave no indication of time or place of posting, which was applied by a separate hand-stamp on the back of the letter.

A Dockwra mark (left). Below is a letter of 1702 with a Bishop mark.

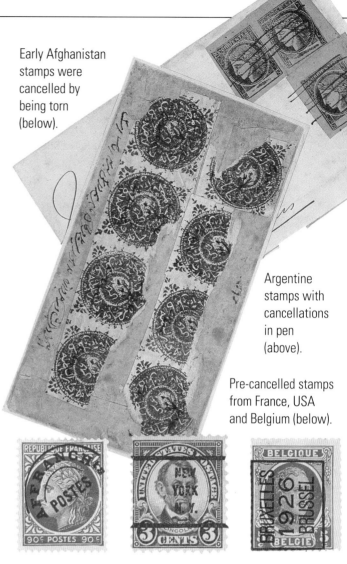

Early Afghanistan stamps were cancelled by being torn (below).

Argentine stamps with cancellations in pen (above).

Pre-cancelled stamps from France, USA and Belgium (below).

UNUSUAL POSTMARKS

There are many other types of postmark applied by postal administrations. These can indicate that there is extra postage to pay, give the reason for delay or damage, show why a letter was undeliverable, or indicate some other interesting aspect of the postal service. In France and some other countries, stamps are issued with a 'postmark' already printed on them. Known as pre-cancels, they are used by posters of bulk quantities of mail.

The 'Maltese Cross' cancel was first struck in red. It was later changed to black.

MODERN CANCELLATIONS

Today, many date-stamp and cancellation devices are combined, the cancellation taking the form of lines or an advertising slogan. Pictorial cancellations are often produced for special occasions - for example, the first day of a stamp issue, an exhibition, anniversary or other important event. Such postmarks should not be overlooked by thematic collectors, because they can make a useful addition to a thematic collection.

Slogan postmarks (above) can make a thematic collection more interesting.

Look for covers (top and centre) with interesting markings. Special postmarks (above) are produced to mark many events.

Heavily postmarked stamps like these (left) should not be included in your collection.

COLLECTOR'S HINT
Never remove a stamp from its envelope unless you are sure that the postmark is of no interest. Early covers, and those from small and remote territories, are often best kept intact.

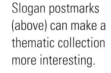
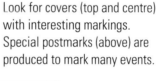
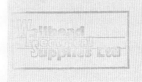

METER MARKS

Meter marks are applied by machines operated by private users licensed by a post office. They combine a 'stamp', date-stamp, and often an advertising slogan. Similar in appearance are automatic stamps (see page 31), such as the French and Norwegian ones below.

OVERPRINTS

An inscription or some other feature added to the design side of a stamp is known as an overprint. There are many reasons why a stamp might be overprinted. For example, a country which has no stamps of its own may use those of another country. The first stamps issued by the island of Cyprus were produced by overprinting those of Great Britain. A country's stamps may also be overprinted to indicate a change of name or status.

SPECIAL ISSUES

Overprinting can be used to produce special stamp issues. This may change an everyday stamp into one for official use only, or into a commemorative issue. Commemorative stamps themselves are often overprinted to enhance their original purpose - stamps issued to mark the Olympic Games or World Cups are often overprinted with the names of some of the winning athletes and teams.

This overprint publicized a disastrous hurricane in British Honduras (now Belize). Sales raised funds for relief work.

Fiji stamps have been overprinted for the New Hebrides (above). The overprint is missing from the top stamp.

These overprints were for an event for which there was not time to design a stamp (above left), and made USA stamps valid in the Panama Canal zone.

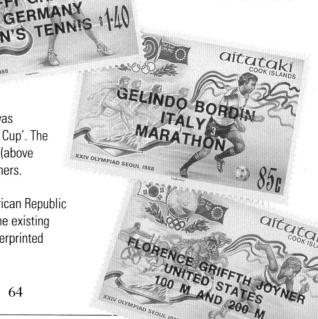

This football stamp (left) was overprinted for the 'French Cup'. The Olympic Games overprints (above and right) name event winners.

When the Central African Republic became an Empire, the existing stamps (left) were overprinted with the new name.

64

SECURITY

Stamps may be overprinted for security purposes. This is often done by companies in order to prevent theft, but has also been carried out by postal authorities. Stamps are sometimes perforated with an initial or a design for the same reason: these are known as 'perfins'. In 1934, Greek letters were included in an airmail overprint on a Macao stamp in order to make forgery difficult.

SURCHARGES

Overprints which include a change of value are known as surcharges. There are many reasons for making surcharges. Stamps may be surcharged because of a shortage of ones of a particular value, perhaps because a new printing has been delayed, or because there has been an increase in postal rates. Sometimes, changes of value are made to use up unwanted stocks of old stamps.

Several of the Commonwealth countries surcharged existing stamps when they changed to a new decimal currency. Surcharges may also be used to raise funds to aid a sudden emergency.

SPECIMENS

Overprinting can also be used to prevent a stamp being used for postal purposes. Stamps are very often overprinted with the words 'cancelled' or 'specimen' (or their foreign equivalent) when they are used for publicity purposes, or when they are distributed to other postal authorities as a reference.

MAKESHIFT OVERPRINTS

Overprints and surcharges are often applied in emergencies by hand-stamps or typeset printing plates. This frequently results in errors such as missing letters, and inverted type. They can also be hand-written or typed, though this does not happen very often.

This stamp from Newfoundland has a hand-written overprinting which includes the Postmaster's initials. The overprinted stamp was intended for use on a pioneering trans-Atlantic flight in 1919.

Commemorative (above left) and charity (above right) surcharges. The Newfoundland stamp has the surcharge inverted.

The three definitive stamps from Gambia, the Netherlands and Zambia (above) have surcharges changing their value. The Gambia stamp has a double surcharge.

An Israeli stamp overprinted 'specimen' (far left), and an Andorran one with the Spanish equivalent, 'Muestra' (left).

65

CINDERELLAS

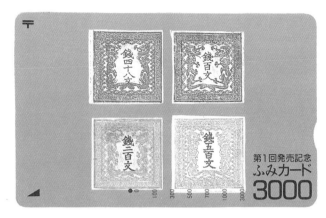

There are many items that look like postage stamps but which you will not find in most stamp catalogues. Some, though performing a limited postal service, have not been issued by a government postal authority; and others are not postage stamps at all. These items are called 'Cinderellas'.

PRIVATE POSTS

Probably the most popular of these Cinderellas are those issued by private companies or local authorities to provide a local service. Produced in limited numbers, they are often difficult to find, especially ones used on covers. Stamps produced by the railway companies which ran the trains before British Rail are much sought after. Some are still issued by many small railway companies today. These railway stamps paid for the carriage of mail on the railway's route. Airline and bus companies have issued similar items.

A Japanese card for buying stamps (above). A telephone bill savings stamp and telegraph stamp (left).

Bogus stamps from the non-existent territories of 'Occussi Ambeno' (left) and 'Sedang' (below).

A railway letter stamp (left) and a cover carried on the Talyllyn Railway (below).

Sara Eade
4 Pretoria Terrace
Castlefields
SHREWSBURY
SY1 2SA

To be posted on arrival at Tywyn

REVENUES

Revenue stamps, issued to collect government taxes and duties, are also keenly collected, especially in the USA. A variety particularly popular with many American collectors are the stamps permitting duck-hunting. Known as 'duck stamps' because their attractive designs depict species of ducks, they have a strong following.

Two 'duck stamps'. The hunter's signature 'cancels' the stamps and makes the hunting permit valid.

Revenue stamps from Belgium (top), Hong Kong (centre) and Malta, the latter being an overprinted postage stamp.

A Zimbabwe airport departure fee stamp (above) valued in US dollars.

These 'local' stamps, right, are from the Norwegian island of Spitzbergen, from Clipperton Island in the north Pacific, and from Lundy in the English Channel.

MISCELLANY

Other items falling into the Cinderella area of collecting are phantom or bogus stamps (those produced for places that do not exist); Christmas seals; postal labels such as those used for airmail or registration purposes; exhibition and other advertising and commemorative labels (especially those connected with philatelic events); and savings stamps; in fact, just about anything that looks like a stamp!

Although many Cinderella items can make unusual additions to a 'normal' stamp collection, they can also be collected in their own right. There is even a special society - the Cinderella Stamp Club - devoted to the study of this interesting aspect of stamp collecting.

Patriotic stamp-like labels from Finland and Denmark (right).

CHRISTMAS POSTS

A recent addition to Cinderella philately are the stamps of the many charity postal services operated at Christmas time in Britain. Often organized by Scout groups, these local services carry Christmas cards at a reduced rate. Special stamps, postmarks and covers are often produced for them.

STAMP CLUBS

Joining a stamp club or philatelic society lets you meet others with a similar hobby and helps you to learn more about philately. Most clubs organize a programme of events that includes visiting speakers, members' displays, competitions and opportunities to swap and buy stamps. Many arrange visits to exhibitions or hold their own. Some publish a newsletter keeping members in touch.

TYPES OF CLUB

Many schools run a stamp club. If yours has one, you should join it, because its members are certain to have an interest in similar subjects to you. You could organize club outings to stamp events and museums, your own competitions and exhibitions, and maybe even your own auction!

Most large towns, too, have a philatelic society. Although these are mainly for adult collectors, some also have a junior section.

The more experienced and expert collector is catered for by specialist societies devoted to the stamps of a particular country, area or thematic subject. There are also countrywide societies: some useful addresses are listed on the next page.

Sorting and soaking stamps at a stamp club meeting can be lots of fun.

STAMP BUG CLUB

The British Post Office runs its own stamp club, the Stamp Bug Club, specially for young collectors, though it has many adult members, too! The club provides members with a colourful magazine several times a year, containing advice, special offers and news, as well as a contact and swaps section. The club does not have regular meetings that collectors can attend, but it is usually present at Britain's two major annual stamp exhibitions (London's Autumn and Spring Stampex) where it organises special activities and there is a chance to meet Stamp Bug himself! Details of the Stamp Bug Club can be obtained from: Stamp Bug Club, FREEPOST, Northampton, NN3 1BR. No stamp is needed on your letter.

Guernsey Post Office's 'First Class' Club offers an exciting starter outfit to new members. It has everything you need to begin collecting stamps, including a special folder.

FINDING A CLUB

Your local library will usually be able to tell you if there is a stamp club near where you live. Your library is also a good source of information about stamp collecting, with books and catalogues often available for loan or reference. Many also have one or more of the monthly stamp magazines for reference.

USEFUL ADDRESSES

You can belong to national stamp clubs as well as to your local club. Here are some useful addresses.

The Australian Post Office (Australia Post, Australian Philatelic Bureau, GPO Box 9988, Melbourne, Victoria 3001, Australia) produces a magazine, *The Stamp Explorer*, for young collectors. It is available from Reply Paid, Stamp Explorer, PO Box 511, South Melbourne, Victoria 3205.

Canada Post's club for young stamp collectors is The Stamp Travellers Club, Canada Post Corporation, Antigonish, Nova Scotia, Canada B2G 2R8.

Great Britain: The National Philatelic Society and the British Philatelic Federation, both at 107 Charterhouse Street, London, Great Britain EC1M 6PT, can provide details of local clubs and societies.

Guernsey's stamp club is the First Class Stamp Club, Guernsey Post Office, Postal Headquarters, Guernsey, Channel Islands

New Zealand Post produces a free bulletin, *Focus*, for collectors of all ages. Send your name and address with a request to be placed on the mailing list to: Basil Umuroa, Manager, Philatelic Bureau New Zealand Post Ltd, Private Bag, Wanganui, New Zealand.

United States of America: The Junior Philatelists of America, P.O. Box 701010, San Antonio, Texas 78270, USA, will send membership information to young collectors who send a large self-addressed stamped envelope.

FOREIGN ALPHABETS

One of the pleasures of collecting stamps is the glimpse they give of life in foreign lands. You will soon notice that many countries use a different name from those we use. Ireland, for example, is Eire, Switzerland calls itself Helvetia. Some countries do not even use the same alphabet that we do.

GREEK AND CYRILLIC

Most countries in Europe, as well as many elsewhere, use the Latin alphabet - the type of letters used in this book. Two other alphabets are also used on stamps in Europe, however, and both contain letters similar to those in the Latin alphabet, as well as some that are not so familiar.

The first of these is Greek, which may be found on the stamps of Greece and Cyprus. The name on Greek stamps translates as Ellas, and a Latin alphabet equivalent of this - Hellas - appears on modern Greek stamps.

The three stamps above left, from Mongolia, the former USSR and Yugoslavia, have Cyrillic inscriptions. The other two stamps are from Greece.

The second alphabet is Cyrillic, an adaptation of Greek. You'll find this alphabet used on the stamps of what was the USSR (Union of Soviet Socialist Republics - Russia in catalogues): the Cyrillic looks like the letters CCCP. You will also find Cyrillic used on stamps from Bulgaria, Mongolia and Yugoslavia.

ALPHABETS OF THE WORLD

αβγδεζηθικλμνξοπορσςτυφφχψω
ΑΒΓΔΕΖΗΘΙΚΛΜΝΞΟΠΟΡΣΤΥΦΧ
ΨΩ 1234567890 .,;;!?

Οἱ πρῶτες ἐκδόσεις ἑλληνικῶν κειμένων ἔγιναν στό τυπο εἷο τοῦ Ἄλδου Μανουτίου στή Βενετία. Ἀπο τό 1494 ὡς τό

Greek

абвгдежзийклмнопрстуфхцчшщъыьэ
юя АБВГДЕЖЗИЙКЛМНОПРСТУФХ
ЦЧШЩЪЫЬЭЮЯ 1234567890 .,;;!?

Азот является одним из главных элементов входящих в состав ве ществ, сбразующих живое тело растений и животных. В процесса

Cyrillic

ابتثجححخدذرزسشصصضطظععغفقكلمنهوىلا
١٢٣٤٥٦٧٨٩٠

فجهاز السي آر ترونيك ٢٠٠ لايعتمد في تصويره لأشكال الحروف ، على عدسات أو مرايا أو قطع ميكانيكية متحركة

Arabic

किसी जाति के जीवन में उसके द्वारा प्रयुक्त शब्दों का अत्यंत महत्त्वपूर्ण स्थान है । आवश्यकता तथा स्थिति के अनुसार इन प्रयुक्त शब्दों का आगम

Indian

OTHER ALPHABETS

Arabic scripts can be found on stamps from many places - from Mauritania in West Africa to Afghanistan in Asia. Fortunately, most of these also carry a Latin alphabet version of their name, making identification easier. So, too, do the stamps of Ethiopia, Israel, India, Thailand and other countries which have their own scripts.

The same cannot be said for many stamps of China, Japan and Korea, whose strange characters often appear very similar to Western eyes. Modern stamps from these countries do often carry a Latin alphabet version of their name - 'Nippon', for example, shows that a stamp is from Japan. The items shown on these pages should help you to sort out earlier stamps from these countries.

Stamps with Arabic (right) and Hebrew (far right) scripts. The stamp below is from South Korea.

Stamps from India are bilingual.

This Japanese stamp can be identified by the chrysanthemum symbol.

A stamp from the Himalayan kingdom of Bhutan.

Chinese stamps. Note the 中 character. Those above are from Taiwan.

STAMPS WITHOUT NAMES

When Great Britain issued the Penny Black in 1840, there was no need for the country name to be on it as no other countries had stamps. Many other early stamps were also issued without a country name. This still continues today on British stamps, though each bears the reigning monarch's head as a means of identification.

Some countries are identified by their initials. USA for United States of America is well-known; other examples include RSA (Republic of South Africa), SWA (South West Africa, now Namibia), DDR (Deutsche Demokratische Republic, better known as East Germany) and KSA (Kingdom of Saudi Arabia). Stamps from Saudi Arabia now carry the country's emblem - a palm tree and crossed scimitars - as a symbol of recognition.

A British stamp showing King George VI.

A greetings stamp from the United States of America (USA).

The palm tree emblem identifies this Saudi Arabian stamp.

A stamp from the former German Democratic Republic (DDR).

British stamps have never had a country name. They are identified by the monarch's head.

STAMP MAPS

Unless you are very good at geography, or have travelled a lot, you probably will not know the names of and where to find all the stamp-issuing countries of the world. The maps provided here can be used with catalogues and printed stamp albums to help organize your collection. The maps show present-day stamp-issuing countries. Also, where the name in English is significantly different from the name in a country's own language, the maps show that country's name as it appears on its stamps. The names in brackets are names used previously by those countries.

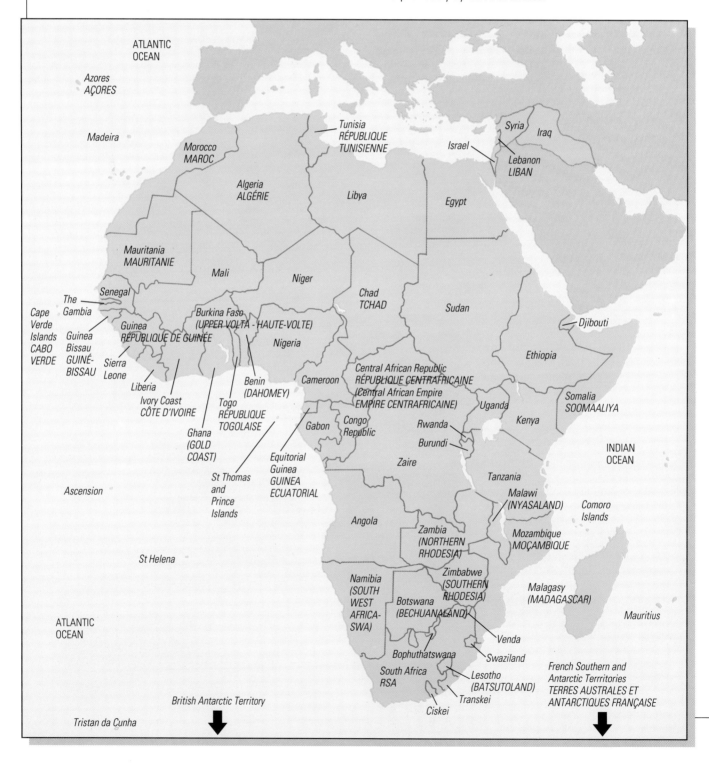

ATLANTIC OCEAN

Azores
AÇORES

Madeira

Morocco
MAROC

Tunisia
RÉPUBLIQUE
TUNISIENNE

Syria
Iraq

Israel
Lebanon
LIBAN

Algeria
ALGÉRIE

Libya

Egypt

Mauritania
MAURITANIE

Mali

Niger

Chad
TCHAD

Sudan

Djibouti

Cape
Verde
Islands
CABO
VERDE

The
Gambia

Senegal

Guinea
Bissau
GUINÉ-
BISSAU

Guinea
RÉPUBLIQUE DE GUINÉE

Burkina Faso
(UPPER VOLTA - HAUTE-VOLTE)

Nigeria

Ethiopia

Somalia
SOOMAALIYA

Sierra
Leone

Liberia

Ivory Coast
CÔTE D'IVOIRE

Togo
RÉPUBLIQUE
TOGOLAISE

Benin
(DAHOMEY)

Cameroon

Central African Republic
RÉPUBLIQUE CENTRAFRICAINE
(Central African Empire
EMPIRE CENTRAFRICAINE)

Uganda

Kenya

Ghana
(GOLD
COAST)

Gabon

Congo
Republic

Rwanda

Burundi

Ascension

St Thomas
and
Prince
Islands

Equitorial
Guinea
GUINEA
ECUATORIAL

Zaire

Tanzania

INDIAN
OCEAN

Malawi
(NYASALAND)

Comoro
Islands

St Helena

Angola

Zambia
(NORTHERN
RHODESIA)

Mozambique
MOÇAMBIQUE

Namibia
(SOUTH
WEST
AFRICA-
SWA)

Botswana
(BECHUANALAND)

Zimbabwe
(SOUTHERN
RHODESIA)

Malagasy
(MADAGASCAR)

Mauritius

ATLANTIC
OCEAN

Venda

Bophuthatswana

Swaziland

South Africa
RSA

Lesotho
(BATSUTOLAND)

French Southern and
Antarctic Terrritories
TERRES AUSTRALES ET
ANTARCTIQUES FRANÇAISE

British Antarctic Territory

Transkei

Ciskei

Tristan da Cunha

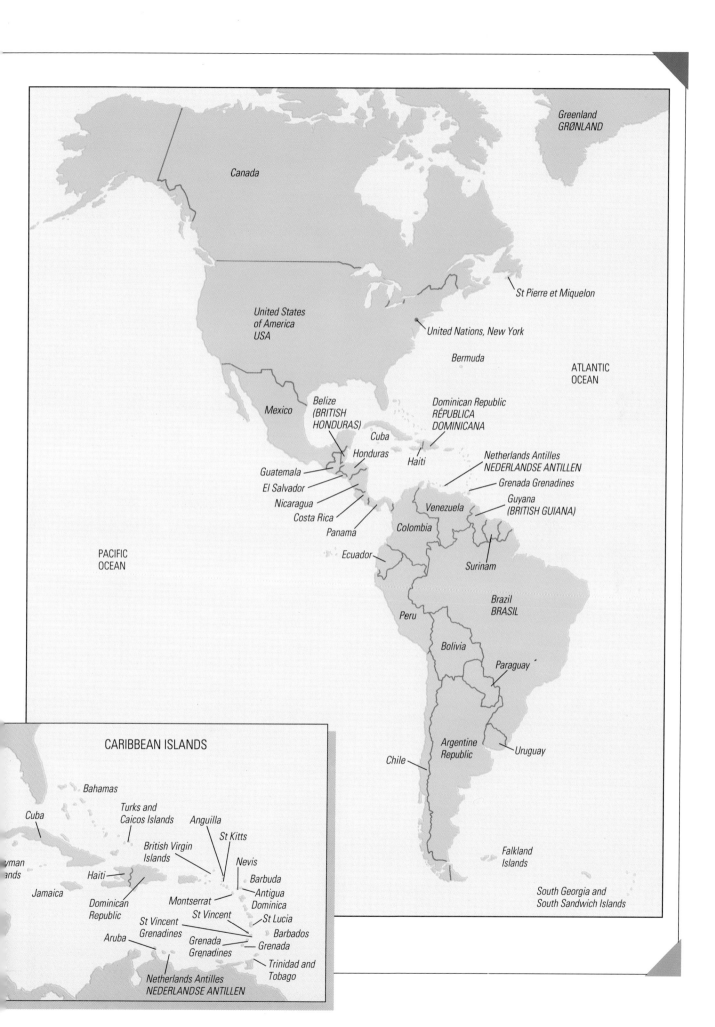

Greenland
GRØNLAND

Canada

United States
of America
USA

St Pierre et Miquelon

United Nations, New York

Bermuda

ATLANTIC
OCEAN

Mexico

Belize
(BRITISH
HONDURAS)

Cuba

Dominican Republic
RÉPUBLICA
DOMINICANA

Honduras

Haiti

Netherlands Antilles
NEDERLANDSE ANTILLEN

Guatemala

Grenada Grenadines

El Salvador

Nicaragua

Venezuela

Guyana
(BRITISH GUIANA)

Costa Rica

Panama

Colombia

PACIFIC
OCEAN

Ecuador

Surinam

Peru

Brazil
BRASIL

Bolivia

Paraguay

Argentine
Republic

Uruguay

Chile

Falkland
Islands

South Georgia and
South Sandwich Islands

CARIBBEAN ISLANDS

Bahamas

Cuba

Turks and
Caicos Islands

Anguilla

St Kitts

British Virgin
Islands

Nevis

yman
ands

Haiti

Barbuda

Antigua

Jamaica

Montserrat

Dominica

Dominican
Republic

St Vincent

St Lucia

St Vincent
Grenadines

Barbados

Aruba

Grenada
Grenadines

Grenada

Netherlands Antilles
NEDERLANDSE ANTILLEN

Trinidad and
Tobago

ATLANTIC
OCEAN

Iceland
ISLAND

Faroe Islands
FØROYAR

Sweden
SVERIGE

Finland
SUOMI FINLAND

Norway
NORGE
or NOREG

Åland
Islands

Isle
of Man

Denmark
DANMARK

Estonia
EESTI

Russian Federation
РОССИЯ/ROSSIJA
(Soviet Union -
CCCP)

Netherlands
NEDERLAND

Latvia
LATVIJA

Ireland
EIRE

Belgium
BELGIQUE
BELGIË

Lithuania
LIETUVA

Great
Britain

Germany
DEUTSCHE BUNDESPOST
(DEUTSCHE POST or
DEUTSCHES
REICH to 1949)

Poland
POLSKA

Byelorussia

Alderney

Guernsey

Jersey

Luxembourg

Czechoslovakia
CESKOSLOVENSKO

France
RÉPUBLIQUE FRANÇAISE

(East Germany
DDR)

United Nations, Vienna
VEREINTE NATIONEN

Ukraine

Liechtenstein

Switzerland
HELVETIA

Austria
ÖSTERREICH

Hungary
MAGYARORZAG
(MAGYAR POSTA)

Rumania
ROMANA

United Nations,
Geneva
NATIONS UNIES

Slovenia
Italy SLOVENIJA
ITALIA

Croatia
REPUBLIKA HRVATSKA

Monaco

Spain
ESPAÑA

San Marino

Andorra
(French)
POSTES

Yugoslavia
JUGOSLAVIJA

Bulgaria
НРЬЪΛΑΡИЯ

Andorra
(Spanish)
CORREOS

Vatican City
POSTE
VATICANE

Turkey
TÜRKIYE

Portugal

Gibraltar

Albania
SHQIPERIA

Malta

Greece
ΕΛΛΑΣ/HELLAS

Cyprus (Turkish)
KUZEY KIBRIS
TÜRK
CUMHURIYETI

MEDITERRANEAN SEA

Cyprus
(Republic)

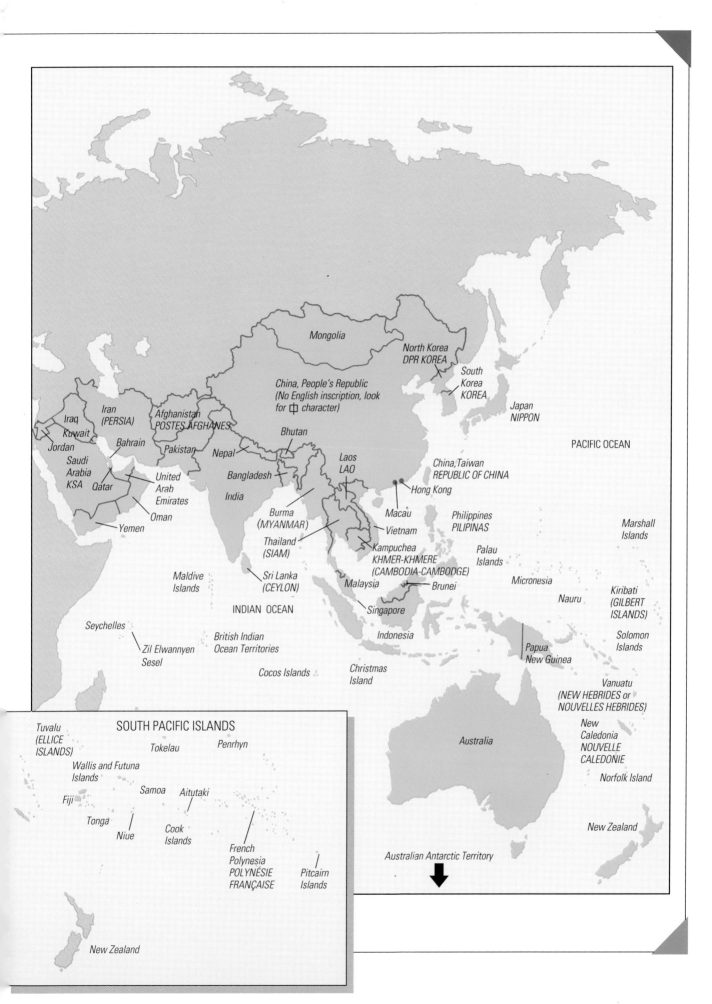

Mongolia

North Korea
DPR KOREA

South
Korea
KOREA

China, People's Republic
(No English inscription, look
for 中 character)

Japan
NIPPON

Iran
(PERSIA)

Iraq

Afghanistan
POSTES AFGHANES

Kuwait

Jordan

Bahrain

Pakistan

Nepal

Bhutan

PACIFIC OCEAN

Saudi
Arabia
KSA

Qatar

United
Arab
Emirates

Bangladesh

India

Laos
LAO

China, Taiwan
REPUBLIC OF CHINA

Hong Kong

Oman

Yemen

Burma
(MYANMAR)

Thailand
(SIAM)

Macau

Vietnam

Philippines
PILIPINAS

Marshall
Islands

Palau
Islands

Maldive
Islands

Sri Lanka
(CEYLON)

Kampuchea
KHMER-KHMERE
(CAMBODIA-CAMBODGE)

Malaysia

Brunei

Micronesia

Nauru

Kiribati
(GILBERT
ISLANDS)

INDIAN OCEAN

Singapore

Solomon
Islands

Seychelles

Zil Elwannyen
Sesel

British Indian
Ocean Territories

Indonesia

Papua
New Guinea

Cocos Islands

Christmas
Island

Vanuatu
(NEW HEBRIDES or
NOUVELLES HEBRIDES)

New
Caledonia
NOUVELLE
CALEDONIE

Australia

Norfolk Island

Australian Antarctic Territory

New Zealand

SOUTH PACIFIC ISLANDS

Tuvalu
(ELLICE
ISLANDS)

Tokelau

Penrhyn

Wallis and Futuna
Islands

Samoa

Aitutaki

Fiji

Tonga

Niue

Cook
Islands

French
Polynesia
POLYNÉSIE
FRANÇAISE

Pitcairn
Islands

New Zealand

INDEX

Italic figures refer to captions or to illustration labels.

adhesive postage stamp 26
    first 8, 54, *54*
aerogramme 26, 32, *32*, 45, *45*, 50, 57
airmail 30, *30*, 33, 38, 56-7, *56*, *57*, 59, *59*, 67
albums 14, 15, *15*, 16, *21*, 23, *23*, 37, 60-1, *61*, 72
aniline 26
anniversaries of stamps *31*
ATMs *32*
auctions 13
automatic stamps *32*, *63*

backstamp 26
balloon mail 56, *56*, 59
banco, 3 skilling 33, *33*
blocks 26, *52*
bogus stamps 26, *66*, 67
booklets 15, 26, *29*, 38, *43*, *44*, 45
'boules de Moulins' *58*, 59
British Guiana one cent 33, *33*
buying stamps *9*, 10-13, *12*

cachet 26
cancellations 26, *37*, 44, 62-3, *62*
catalogues 16, *19*, 24-5, *24*, *25*, 37, 41, *41*, 72
Champion, Theodore 8, *8*
charity stamps 28, *28*, 67
checklists *41*
Christmas posts 67, *67*
Cinderellas 38, 45, 66-7
circular date stamp (CDS) 26
clay letters 54, *54*, *55*
cliché 26
clubs/societies *9*, 11, 12, 67, 68-9, *68*, *69*
coil stamps *29*, *39*
colour guide 18
commemoratives 27, 29, *29*, 64, *64*
'cottonreel' 33, *33*, *51*
country collecting 14, 23, 36-9, 68

covers 23, 26, 38, *38*, *44*, 56, 57, 60-1, *61*, *63*, *66*, 67
CTO (cancelled to order) 26
Cursus Publicus 54, *54*

datestamps 37, 62, 63, *63*
dealers 11, 13, 36, *50*, 51, 60
definitives 28, *28*, 29, 37, *39*, 65
design 27, 28, *28*, 34, 35, *45*, 46, 53, *53*, 60
die plate 26
'duck stamps' 67, *67*

early stamps 31
embossing 26, *34*, 48
envelopes 32, *32*, 35, 38, 45, *45*, 54, 55, 60
    mounting 44
errors *16*, 33, *33*, 35, 38, 45, 47, 52-3, *52*, *53*, 65
essays 26, 47
exhibitions *9*, 13, *31*, 69

facsimiles 26, 51
fairs 11
fakes 51
faults *13*
first day covers 15, *21*, *43*, 60-1, *60*, *61*
first flight covers 57, *57*
flaws *39*, 52, *52*
forgeries 50-1, *50*, *51*, 65
'Framas' *32*
frank/franking 26
'free forms' 34

George V, King 8
Gibbons, Stanley 8, 24, *24*
gramophone record stamps 35, *35*
greetings stamps *29*, 71
gum, original 26
gutter 26

hinges 15, *21*, *21*
holograms 35, *35*

imprint 26
intaglio 26, 47, 48, *48*

'Inverted Curtiss Jenny' 33, *33*
'Inverted Swan' 33, *33*

Jubilee Line 26

key plate/type 26
killer 26
kiloware 10, *10*

letterpress printing *49*
list-keeping *13*
lithographic printing 47, 48, *49*
'local' stamps *67*
London Penny Post 62

magazines 11, 13, 24
magnifying glass *16*, 47, *48*, *49*
'Maltese Cross' cancel 62, *62*
Maxicard 60, *60*
meter mark *32*, 44, *44*, *63*
mint stamps *21*, *25*, 26, 27
'Missing Virgin' 33, *33*
mounts/mounting 10, 15, *20*, 21, *21*, 23, *23*, *29*, *39*, *44*, *61*
mourning stamp *29*
'Mulreadys' 55

new issues 36
note-writing *18*, *22*, *23*, *39*, 43

omnibus issues *29*
overprints *30*, *45*, 50, 57, 64-5, *64*, *65*

pane 26, 37
paper 19, 24, *34*, 35
paquebot 26
Penny Black 13, *48*, 51, 54, *54*, 55, *55*, 60, 62, *71*
perfins 26, 65
perforation 17, 18, 24, *25*, 27, 28, *29*, 46, 51, 52, *53*, 65
perforation gauge 17, *17*
Philatelic Bureau 12, 60
phosphor bands/ink 19, *19*, *25*
photographic printing *49*
photogravure 47, 48, *48*
PHQ card 26
pigeon mail 56, 59
plastic-moulded stamps 35
Pony Express 58
'Postage due' *30*, *32*, 38
postal fiscal 26
postal history 8, *9*, *11*, 38, 54-5, *54*, *55*, 62
postal services 38, *38*, 54
postal stationery 32, 35, 38, 45, *45*, 51, 55
postboxes *11*, *12*
postcards 15, 32, *32*, 45, *45*, 60
Posthorn 28
postmarks *9*, 20, *20*, 23, *32*, 37, 38, *38*, 44, *44*, 50, 51, *51*, 55, 57, 60, *61*, 62, *62*, 63, *63*, 67

'Inverted Curtiss Jenny' 33, *33*
'Inverted Swan' 33, *33*

post offices 12, *12*, 26, 27, 36
'Post Office' Mauritius 31, *31*, *51*
Post Office services stamps 30, *30*
pre-cancels 26, 62, *62*
preparing stamps *20*
printing materials 35
printing methods *16*, 47-9, *48*, *49*
prismatic-ribbed stamps 35
production 8, 47

railway stamps *30*, 66, *66*
rarities 31, *31*, 33, *33*, *51*
re-entry 27
regional stamps 28
revenue stamps *67*, 67
'rocket mail' *59*
roll-printing 47
Roosevelt, President 8
rouletting *47*
runner post 58

savings stamps *66*, 67
scented stamps 35
Scott, John 8, *24*
selvedge 27
'se tenant' stamps *27*, 35, *52*
shapes 34, *34*
sheet-printing 47
single-issue collecting 37
slogan cancels/postmarks 37, 44, *44*, *45*, 63, *63*,
special issues 64, *64*
specimens 65, *65*
stamp packets 10, *10*, 11
stamps on stamps *31*
stockbooks 15, 21, *21*
strip 27
surcharges 65, *65*

tab 27
'tête-bêche' *35*
thematic collecting 14, 23, *29*, 40-3, *41*, *43*, *44*, 45, 63, *63*, 68
themes 8, *9*, 24, *31*, 40, *41*, 42
three-dimensionals (3-D) 35, *35*
'tin can mail' 59, *59*
traffic lights 27, *27*
transit mark 27
tweezers *16*, 20

Universal Postal Union 27
varieties *16*, 38, 45
vending machines *12*, *32*
vignette 27

War Tax stamp *30*
watermarks 18, *19*, 24, 28, *39*, *45*, 51
wing margin 27
'Woodblocks' 33, *33*